T4-AUZ-443

NORTON COMMANDER MODE

Panel

Scroll bar

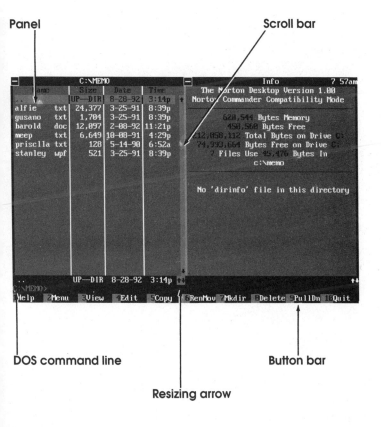

		C:\MEMO					Info	7 57am
	Name	Size	Date	Time		The Norton Desktop Version 1.00		
..		UP—DIR	8-28-92	3:14p		Norton Commander Compatibility Mode		
alfie	txt	24,377	3-25-91	8:39p				
gusano	txt	1,704	3-25-91	8:39p		620,544 Bytes Memory		
harold	doc	12,097	2-08-92	11:21p		450,560 Bytes Free		
meep	txt	6,649	10-08-91	4:29p		12,058,112 Total Bytes on Drive C:		
prisclla	txt	128	5-14-90	6:52a		74,993,664 Bytes Free on Drive C:		
stanley	wpf	521	3-25-91	8:39p		7 Files Use 45,476 Bytes In		
						c:\memo		
						No 'dirinfo' file in this directory		

.. UP—DIR 8-28-92 3:14p

C:\MEMO>

1Help 2Menu 3View 4Edit 5Copy 6RenMov 7Mkdir 8Delete 9PullDn 10Quit

DOS command line

Button bar

Resizing arrow

The SYBEX Instant Reference Series

Instant References are available on these topics:

AutoCAD Release 11

AutoCAD Release 12

dBASE

dBASE III PLUS Programming

dBASE IV Programming

dBASE IV 1.1

DESQview

DOS

DOS 5

Excel 4 for Windows

Harvard Graphics 3

Harvard Graphics for Windows

Lotus 1-2-3 Release 2.3

Lotus 1-2-3 for Windows

Macintosh Software

Microsoft Word for the Macintosh

Microsoft Word for the PC

Norton Desktop for Windows

Norton Utilities 6

PageMaker 4.0 for the Macintosh

Paradox 3.5

Paradox 4.0

PC Tools 7.1

Quattro Pro 3

Windows 3.0

Windows 3.1

Word for Windows, Version 2.0

WordPerfect 5

WordPerfect 5.1

WordPerfect 5.1 for Windows

Computer users are not all alike.
Neither are SYBEX books.

We know our customers have a variety of needs. They've told us so. And because we've listened, we've developed several distinct types of books to meet the needs of each of our customers. What are you looking for in computer help?

If you're looking for the basics, try the **ABC's** series. For a more visual approach, select full-color **Quick & Easy** books.

Running Start books are two books in one: a fast-paced tutorial, followed by a command reference.

Mastering and **Understanding** titles offer you a step-by-step introduction, plus an in-depth examination of intermediate-level features, to use as you progress.

Our **Up & Running** series is designed for computer-literate consumers who want a no-nonsense overview of new programs. Just 20 basic lessons, and you're on your way.

SYBEX **Encyclopedias, Desktop References,** and **A to Z** books provide a *comprehensive reference* and explanation of all of the commands, features, and functions of the subject software.

Sometimes a subject requires a special treatment that our standard series don't provide. So you'll find we have titles like **Advanced Techniques, Handbooks, Tips & Tricks,** and others that are specifically tailored to satisfy a unique need.

You'll find SYBEX publishes a variety of books on every popular software package. Looking for computer help? Help Yourself to SYBEX.

For a complete catalog of our publications:

SYBEX SYBEX Inc.
2021 Challenger Drive, Alameda, CA 94501
Tel: (510) 523-8233/(800) 227-2346 Telex: 336311
Fax: (510) 523-2373

Norton Desktop™
for DOS® Instant Reference

Sharon Crawford

Charlie Russel

SYBEX®

San Francisco • Paris • Düsseldorf • Soest

Acquisitions Editor: Dianne King
Developmental Editor: James A. Compton
Project Editor: Barbara Dahl
Editor: Jon Britton
Technical Editor: Dean Denno
Word Processors: Ann Dunn, Chris Meredith
Series Book Designer: Ingrid Owen
Desktop Publishing Production: Lisa Jaffe
Screen Graphics: Aldo Bermudez, Cuong Le
Production Assistant: David Silva
Indexer: Nancy Guenther
Cover Designer: Archer Design
Screen reproductions produced with Collage Plus.
Collage Plus is a trademark of Inner Media Inc.

SYBEX is a registered trademark of SYBEX Inc.

TRADEMARKS: SYBEX has attempted throughout this book to distinguish proprietary trademarks from descriptive terms by following the capitalization style used by the manufacturer.

SYBEX is not affiliated with any manufacturer.

Every effort has been made to supply complete and accurate information. However, SYBEX assumes no responsibility for its use, nor for any infringement of the intellectual property rights of third parties which would result from such use.

Library of Congress Card Number: 92-61599
ISBN: 0-7821-1193-9

Manufactured in the United States of America
10 9 8 7 6 5 4 3 2 1

Acknowledgments

Our thanks to Michael Gross, author of *Norton Utilities 6.0 Instant Reference*, who supplied us with considerable material, all of it well written. His generous contribution made this book possible.

Appreciation and gratitude are due to all the hard-working folk at Sybex who, on a daily basis, turn sows' ears into silk purses without batting an eye. In particular, thanks to (in order of appearance in the process) Dianne King, Gary Masters, Barbara Dahl, Lisa Jaffe, Aldo Bermudez, and David Silva.

Thanks also to editor Jon Britton and technical editor Dean Denno. They found and corrected our errors at a rate that was comforting and annoying all at the same time.

Table of Contents

Introduction

xiii

Part One

Installation and Memory Considerations

Installing Norton Desktop for DOS   2

Memory Considerations   9

Part Two

Configuring the Desktop

BUTTON BAR   18

CLOCK   19

COMPRESSION   19

CONFIRMATION   21

DESKTOP LINK   21

EDITOR   23

MOUSE   24

NETWORK   25

PASSWORDS   26

PREFERENCES   27

PRINTER   30

PULL-DOWN MENUS   32

SCREEN   37

SCREEN SAVER/SLEEPER   41

SAVE CONFIGURATION   43

SHUTDOWN ROUTINE   43

STARTUP PROGRAMS   45

Part Three
Managing Files

ASSOCIATING A FILE   50
ATTRIBUTES   52
COMPRESS   53
COPY   54
DELETE   55
EDITING FILES   56
FIND/SUPERFIND   60
LAUNCHING FILES   65
MAKE DIRECTORY   67
MOVE   67
OPENING FILES   68
PRINTING FILES   68
PROPERTIES   69
PRUNE AND GRAFT   70
RENAME   71
RUN   71
SELECT AND DESELECT   71
VIEWING FILES   72
WINDOWS   75

Part Four
Tools and Utilities

CALCULATOR   84
CALENDAR   85
LINK PCs   85
DISKETTE FUNCTIONS   87
NORTON MAIL   91
NORTON MENU   102

NETWORK MESSAGE   111
NORTON ANTIVIRUS   112
NORTON BACKUP   120
NORTON DISK DOCTOR   147
SCHEDULER   152
SPEED DISK   155
SYSTEM INFORMATION   164
UNERASE   168

Part Five

Standalone Programs

ADVISE   182
DISK TOOLS   183
IMAGE   187
NORTON CACHE   188
SMARTCAN   193
UNFORMAT   196

Appendix A

Batch Enhancer

200

Appendix B

Running in Norton Commander Mode

209

Index

213

Introduction

Norton Desktop for DOS combines an uncomplicated, visual interface with an assortment of helpful tools that even a nontechnical user will find easy to use. Files can be viewed, copied, moved, and edited with a few keystrokes or clicks of a mouse. Programs can be run from a menu or by selecting them in a window.

HOW THIS BOOK IS ORGANIZED

This book is organized into five sections. In Part One, we cover the installation and memory options available. Norton Desktop for DOS must be installed correctly for the user to get the maximum benefit, and speed can be greatly enhanced through proper configuration.

Part Two, "Configuring the Desktop," covers the many options for setting up the look and operation of the desktop. Virtually every detail of the program can be configured to suit the way you work.

Part Three, "Managing Files," covers the routine operations that can be so confusing in DOS and are so simple in the Norton Desktop for DOS. Find, copy, compress, move, and print files with ease. Here you will find clear instructions on how to open drive windows, change file attributes, and make directories.

Part Four, "Tools and Utilities," includes step-by-step guidance on how to use Norton Backup, Norton AntiVirus, UnErase, and the other valuable tools in the package. Also covered are the Norton Menus, which can help you efficiently organize your work.

Part Five, "Standalone Programs," covers useful utilities such as Image and Norton Cache that can both safeguard your work and optimize your computer's performance.

Two appendices are included. One covers the Batch Enhancer commands, useful tools in building batch files. The other gives instructions on running the program in Norton Commander mode, a desktop style with commands compatible with the program Norton Commander 3.0.

NAVIGATING THE DESKTOP

All the commands and operations in Norton Desktop for DOS can be accessed easily using the keyboard, mouse, or combination of both. In this book, instructions are given to "select" or "click on" an item. How you select an item depends on whether you are using a mouse or a keyboard. The following sections describe both as well as the parts of the desktop.

Using a Mouse

To click on an item, position the mouse pointer over that item, then press and release the left mouse button once. Double-clicking means that you position the pointer and press the mouse button twice in rapid succession.

To drag an item, click on it and hold down the mouse button. When you move the mouse, you will see the item pulled along the screen. When you reach the place where you want the item to go, release the mouse button.

To select an item from a menu, click on the menu name. While holding down the mouse button, move the mouse until it highlights the item you want, then release the button. You can also select an item from a menu by clicking once on the menu's name and once on the item.

To select multiple items from a list, click the right mouse button. To select a contiguous sequence of files, click on the first file with the right mouse button and drag the mouse to the last item you want to select. Release the button.

Using the Keyboard

You pull down menus by pressing the Alt key and the letter that is a contrasting color in the menu name. When the menu is visible, key in the contrasting letter in the command name to make your selection. Or you can use the ↓ or ↑ key to move the highlight to your choice and press Enter. Inside dialog boxes, move the highlight using the Tab key or the arrow keys.

See Table I.1 for a list of the most common keyboard commands.

Table I.1: The Most Common Keyboard Commands

Action	Keyboard
Activate an open window	Ctrl+Tab. Repeat until window is highlighted.
Close a control menu	Esc
Close a drive window	Ctrl+F4
Move an open window	Select Move from control menu. Use arrow keys. Press Enter when finished.
Open a control menu	Alt+- or Esc
Close a drop-down list box	Ctrl+↑
Open a drop-down list box	Ctrl+↓
Resize a drive window	Choose Size from the control menu. Use the arrow keys to adjust the size and press Enter.
Restore a maximized drive window to original size	Select Restore from control menu
Select all files	Ctrl+/
Deselect all files	Ctrl+\
Select multiple files	Use arrows to highlight the file and press Insert. Repeat for additional files.

Menus

In the Norton Desktop, there is a menu bar with the names of the menus at the top of the screen. Click on the name of the menu, and the listing will appear below it. By default, the program opens with the short version of the menus. To see the full listing, you must select Long Pull-downs from the Configure menu.

Menu names include other indications as to their functions. For example, an ellipsis (…) following a menu name signifies that choosing that item will open a dialog box with additional choices. A solid triangle (➤) after an item means that a submenu will appear when that item is highlighted.

Some menu items, such as the first three items under the View menu, are toggles. (A toggled item is alternately turned off and on each time you select it.) When you select one of these, a check mark will appear indicating that the function is on. When you click on the item again, the check mark will disappear and the function will be toggled off.

Functions that are dimmed are not available for use. For example, the Network Message function in the Tools menu is dimmed unless you are on a network.

BOXES AND BUTTONS

Many of the operations in Norton Desktop for DOS must be done by means of various boxes and buttons. It may seem that there are many names for similar functions, but you should familiarize yourself with these names because they signify how the box or button can be used.

Browse Box   When you select a browse button, a browse box will open. It usually includes file, directory, and drive windows, so you can locate files whose exact name or location you may not remember. When you find and select the file and then click on OK, the file's name will appear in the original dialog box. A double-click on the file's name will have the same result.

Check Box   A square box next to an item is a check box that can be turned on or off. To select that item, click on the square box. An X or a check mark will appear to indicate that the item is toggled on. To turn the choice off, select the square box again and the box will clear.

Speed-Search Box   A speed-search box is the quickest way to find a file or directory in a Tree Pane or File Pane. When you start typing the name of the file or directory, the speed-search box appears below the active pane and the cursor bar moves to highlight the first file or directory that matches the letters typed. When the cursor bar has moved to the file or directory you want, press Enter to select it.

Tri-State Box   A tri-state box is just like a check box except that it has three settings. If there is an X in the box, the option is turned on. If the setting is blank, the option is turned off. If the box contains a solid rectangle, the program will disregard whether the option is on or off.

Text Box   A text box is a blank box where you key in text or numbers. Click anywhere in the text box and a blinking cursor will appear at the left side of the box. Begin keying in text at the cursor. To make a change in your text, press the Backspace key.

Drop-Down Box   A drop-down box is a text box with a choice already in it and a prompt button on the right side of the box. Click the prompt button, and the box will open downward and reveal other choices you can select.

Combination Box   A combination box looks and acts like a drop-down box, except that in addition to the choices provided, you can also key in your own choice.

Dialog Box   A dialog box is a window that allows you to select the options available for the program or function chosen. The term dialog box is used often and refers to any box with user choices. Dialog boxes always appear when you choose a menu command that contains an ellipsis (...).

Control Box   The control box is at the upper left-hand corner of the main Norton Desktop menu bar and all other windows and dialog boxes. It is a dark box with a slotlike mark. To see the Control menu, click on the control box with the mouse or press Alt+-.

Command Button   When selected, a command button causes the program to execute an action. Command buttons include OK, Cancel, Select, Browse, and so forth. They are rectangularly shaped, and when they are selected they appear to depress.

The Minimize and Restore Buttons   At the upper right-hand corner of some windows is a button with either an up or down arrow. Click on the upward-pointing arrow, or select Maximize from the Control menu, to enlarge the window to full-height screen size. The arrow then points down. Click on it, or select Restore from the Control menu, to return the window to its previous size.

Prompt Button   A prompt button is located on the right side of a drop-down or combination box. It has a down-pointing arrow on it indicating that you can click or press Ctrl+↓ to make more choices available.

Radio Button   Radio buttons function just like the selection buttons on a radio. Only one can be on at a time. To select one is to deselect any other. Usually, a radio button is round, and when it is toggled on, its center darkens.

BARS

Bars appear on dialog boxes and other windows. The title bar, menu bar, and scroll bars provide information on the window's function and contents.

Title Bar   The title bar appears at the top of every window and box. The name of the program or dialog box is written there. To move a window, click on the title bar and drag the window to the location you choose.

Menu Bar   The menu bar is just below the title bar. Only the titles of available menus appear on the menu bar. When you select a menu name, a list appears with any currently unavailable items dimmed.

Scroll Bar   Whenever the information in a window will not fit into the available space, the window will have a scroll bar on its right edge. To move up or down in the window, click the up or down arrow. To move more rapidly, click and drag the slider box in the scroll bar.

Some windows will also have horizontal scroll bars that work in the same manner except that they move from side to side.

WILDCARDS

Norton Desktop for DOS recognizes the following wildcard characters:

?   Represents a single character at the corresponding position.

*   Represents all the remaining characters in the field.

| Represents one or zero characters.

Entries in this book specify those cases where wildcards cannot be used.

● EXAMPLES

BUDGET.PR?   Represents all files with the name BUDGET where the extension begins with the letters *PR*, but any character can be in the third position.

BUDGET.*   Represents all files with the name BUDGET with any extension.

| |**.PRN**   Represents all files with the extension PRN that also have two or fewer characters in their names.

Part One

Installation and Memory Considerations

The Norton Desktop for DOS includes a sophisticated and flexible installation program that must be used to install Desktop onto your hard disk. This installation program can be used to simply copy and extract the programs files onto your hard disk, or you can also use it to preconfigure many of the tools included with the Desktop. You can choose to control each aspect of this process, or let it do its work virtually automatically, requiring little from you except occasionally pressing the Enter key or changing floppy disks.

● **WARNING**   Do not attempt to install the Norton Desktop for DOS if you have deleted files that you need to recover, or have accidentally formatted your hard disk. Instead, insert the Emergency–Data Recovery disk into a floppy drive, and run the Unerase or Unformat programs from that disk. For more information on these programs, see "Unerase" in Part Four or "Unformat" in Part Five.

INSTALLING NORTON DESKTOP FOR DOS

Norton Desktop for DOS provides for three levels of installation: Full, Minimal, and Custom. The custom installation procedure is recommended even if you plan on installing all of the Norton Desktop for DOS. This procedure not only gives you more control over which tools are installed, it also lets you select which tools you want to preconfigure. If you have limited hard-disk space, you may select Minimal Install, but here again, we recommend that you use the custom installation option to both preserve your options and allow you to preconfigure the components you do select. If you do select either Full Install or Minimal Install, several of the steps described below will be bypassed. Pay particular attention, however, to steps 12 and 13, which describe modifying your startup files.

To Install Norton Desktop for DOS

1.   Insert Disk 1 into the appropriate floppy-disk drive.

2.   Key in **a:install**. If the disk is in drive B, substitute **b:** for **a:**.

3.   The install program may ask you to choose Color, Black & White, or Laptop color palettes and will then show a warning screen about not installing if you want to recover erased files or a formatted hard disk. Press Enter to proceed.

4. This is followed by one or more information screens. Again, press Enter to continue.

5. The install program will then use Norton AntiVirus to scan your computer's memory and boot disk for a virus.

6. Next it will pop up a personalization screen. You must key in a name here, and you may key in a company name as well. Press Enter to proceed.

7. Finally, the Install screen pops up. Full Install will be highlighted. Use the cursor keys to highlight Custom Install, and then press the Enter key to begin installation, or click on Custom Install with your mouse.

8. Key in the directory to which you wish to install Norton Desktop for DOS, or press Enter to accept the default.

9. The Install Program Files screen pops up. Select the programs you wish to install, using the cursor keys or your mouse to highlight the individual programs, and then either press the spacebar or click with the mouse to select the programs. As shown in Figure 1.1, a check appears to the left of programs that will be installed.

10. Select Install to begin the installation. If there is insufficient space on the drive you have selected, and you want to change drives, select New Drive to change to a different destination drive. Select Return to DOS to cancel the installation and return to the DOS prompt.

11. Next, select the tools to be added to your startup files, and the ones you want to preconfigure during the installation. Estimates of the time it will take to configure the options are shown on the right-hand side. Items that are selected are checked on the left-hand side. When finished, press Enter or select Continue. Installer will copy files to your hard disk, requesting program diskettes as needed.

12. The Save System Files screen opens next. This shows you the changes to your startup files that you selected in the Select Configuration Options screen. You can make changes to those selections in the bottom window of this screen, as shown in Figure 1.2. Check whether you want Norton Installer to make the changes directly to your

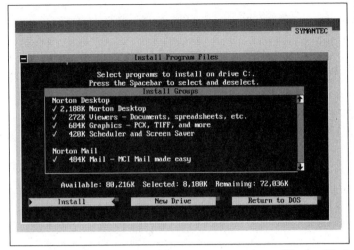

Figure 1.1: The Norton Installer checks options that will be installed.

AUTOEXEC.BAT and CONFIG.SYS files for you, save the
changes to sample files in your Norton Desktop directory,
or make no changes. We recommend that you save the
changes to alternate files.

13. Select Review from the Save System Files screen. This
brings up the Editing Startup Files screen. Initially the
recommended changes to your AUTOEXEC.BAT file are
shown. You can move or delete an individual line by
highlighting it with the cursor keys, or clicking on it with
the mouse, and selecting Move or Delete. If you select
Move, the line will follow the cursor; when the cursor is
where you want the line, select Drop. To see the recommended changes to your CONFIG.SYS file, press Alt+F,
followed by Ctrl+↓, ↓, Enter. Or click on the down arrow
at the end of the File line with your mouse, then click on
the file you want to see. When you are satisfied with the
changes, select OK to proceed, and then OK again.

14. If Norton detects that you may have selected programs
that would cause you to use too much memory, it will
warn you that it requires at least 475K of DOS memory
to run. If you get this warning, either press Esc to back up

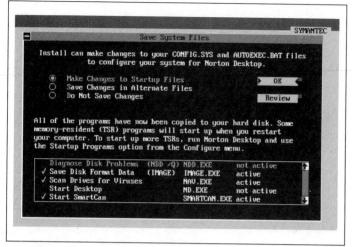

Figure 1.2: Norton Installer can modify your startup files.

and modify your selections, or go ahead and save the changes, and then consult the section on memory management later in this section.

15. Next, if you selected the Create rescue disk option, Norton Disk Tools will create the disk. While this disk doesn't need to be a bootable disk, it is a good idea to use a bootable disk (one formatted with the /s option) when possible. Follow the prompts to save this critical disaster recovery information.

16. If you selected Configure Norton Backup, the Norton Backup configuration program will start next. See "Norton Backup" in Part Four for details about this installation program.

17. Finally, if you selected "Create menus for your programs" in step 11 above, the installer will automatically generate your initial Norton Menu files. This requires no intervention on your part.

18. When the installation is complete, you will be offered the option of rebooting your computer, going straight to the

Norton Desktop program, or simply returning to DOS. If you asked the install program to directly modify your startup files, you should reboot your computer so that these changes can go into effect. If you asked that any changes be saved to alternate files, return to DOS at this point, examine the suggested changes, modify your CONFIG.SYS and AUTOEXEC.BAT files as necessary, and then reboot. Or, simply go directly to Norton Desktop for DOS and use its viewing and editing tools to see the suggested changes, and make them yourself.

● OPTIONS–TOOLS

The custom installation provides you with the opportunity to select or deselect the installation of the various elements of the Norton Desktop for DOS. If you choose not to install a tool during the initial installation, you will need to rerun the installation program to install that tool if you later find you need it.

Norton Desktop   The main program. Always choose this unless you are adding previously skipped components to an already existing installation.

Viewers   Allows you to view word processing, database, and spreadsheet files.

Graphics   Additional viewers that allow you to view graphics files.

Scheduler and Screen Saver   Allows you to schedule events, backups, and so on, automatically, and includes a graphical screen saver.

Mail   Automates the use of MCI Mail. Select only if you have both a modem and an MCI Mail account.

AntiVirus   The full DOS version of the Norton AntiVirus program. Protects against both known viruses and ones that haven't even been created yet.

Backup   The full DOS version of the Norton Backup program. Allows you to quickly and reliably back up your hard disk to floppies or to many QIC-40 and QIC-80 tape drives.

Menus   Allows you to create custom menus to run all your favorite programs without leaving Norton Desktop for DOS.

Norton Disk Doctor   Diagnoses and repairs many disk problems automatically.

UnErase   Unerases accidentally deleted files.

UnFormat   Unformats accidentally formatted hard disks, and floppy disks that have been formatted with a "safe" formatter, including the DOS 5 format program.

Image   Helps protect against data loss if you accidentally format your hard disk.

SmartCan   Helps protect against data loss if you accidentally delete files on your hard disk.

Disk Tools   Powerful disaster recovery and prevention tools.

Norton Cache   Improves the speed of disk access.

Speed Disk   Unfragments the files on your hard disk, improving the speed of disk access and greatly improving your chances of data recovery in case of disk misadventure.

System Information   Diagnostics and benchmarks for your entire computer system.

Safe Format   Quickly and safely formats diskettes, protecting you in case of accidental formatting.

Batch Enhancer Plus   Adds additional features to DOS's batch language.

Installer   The installation program. You must select this.

Norton Configuration Program   Allows you to configure the desktop and utilities after they are installed. You must select this.

README.TXT   A text file with last-minute changes and information. You must select this.

● OPTIONS-PRECONFIGURE

The installation program allows you to preconfigure and automatically load many of the tools included with Norton Desktop for DOS, as well as schedule system maintenance events, such as backups and disk optimization. The choices are:

Run Norton Disk Doctor on startup   Runs a quick check of the health of your hard disk every time you boot your computer.

Run Image on startup   Saves a copy of your File Allocation Table (FAT) every time you boot your computer. *Highly Recommended.*

Run SmartCan on startup   Loads a memory-resident program that helps recover accidentally erased files. Recommended only where memory is not a problem, and accidental erasure is.

Scan for viruses on startup   Automatically scans your hard disk for infection by a virus every time you boot your computer. Recommended in environments susceptible to viral attacks, such as where multiple users have access to the same computer.

Start virus intercept   Loads a device driver that protects against viral attack. *Recommended.*

Start Norton Cache   Loads Norton Cache every time you boot your computer to improve disk access time. Recommended if you have more than 640K of memory available unless you are using another cache that you prefer.

Load Scheduler/Screen Saver   Loads the Scheduler into memory every time you boot your computer. Recommended if you want to be able to have automatic reminders and scheduling of programs and be able to use the screen saver in all DOS applications. This program requires approximately 13K of DOS memory.

Schedule weekly disk optimization   Uses the Scheduler to automatically unfragment the files on your hard disk weekly. We recommend that you do this at least weekly, whether you use the Scheduler or a Shutdown routine to invoke Norton Speed Disk, or do so manually.

Schedule daily backup   Uses the Scheduler to run the Norton Backup automatically every afternoon. Highly recommended if you work with files that you could not afford to lose.

Start Norton Desktop after startup   Loads Norton Desktop every time your start your computer. *Recommended.*

Add the ND directory to the PATH   Adds the Norton Desktop directory to your path so that you can start the desktop from anywhere.

Configure Norton Desktop   Automatically configures Norton Desktop. Required, and can't be unselected.

Create Windows group for Desktop   Automatically creates a Norton Desktop for DOS group the next time you start Microsoft Windows. If you use Windows, select this.

Create a rescue disk after install   Creates a rescue disk containing copies of your CMOS and hard-disk partition table and boot-sector information. This could help you recover from a major disaster. *Highly Recommended*.

Configure Norton Backup   The first time you use Norton Backup, it needs to run a variety of tests to ensure reliable backups. This takes about 15 minutes. Pay now, or pay later, but it needs to be done, regardless.

Create menus for your programs   Automatically detects the programs already on your hard disk, and creates menus for them. *Recommended*.

MEMORY CONSIDERATIONS

The Norton Desktop for DOS requires a minimum of approximately 465K–470K of DOS memory to load and run. This means that the memory shown by running the DOS program CHKDSK should be between 475,000 and 480,000 bytes of memory available. This number will vary slightly depending on what kind of machine you have and what type of memory you have available. This should be considered the barest minimum, however, as some users have reported erratic results with memory configurations near or at the minimum. We recommend that you have at least 500,000 bytes free before starting Norton Desktop for DOS. Given that DOS starts out with approximately 640K of memory, initially, it shouldn't be too hard to make sure that there is enough left over for Norton Desktop. However, if you are running on a network or have other memory-resident programs that are using substantial amounts of memory, and you are running close to or below this minimum, then here are a few tricks to try.

- If you have an 80286 or above computer with at least 1MB of RAM, you should be running under DOS 5. If you aren't, you should upgrade, since you will save a substantial amount of memory over previous versions, especially since most of DOS itself can then be loaded into high memory. More on high memory later.

- If you using an 80386 or 80486 computer, load some of your memory-resident programs into high memory. *All* the possible procedures and tricks for this are beyond the scope of this book, but for some help with loading programs high, and some of the things to watch out for, see "To Load TSRs into High Memory," below.

- If you have an older IBM-PC or IBM-XT compatible, you can still run Norton Desktop for DOS, but your options are a bit more limited. You can't load programs into high memory, and DOS 5 won't gain you very much, but there are still a few tricks available to speed up your computer if you have expanded memory available. See "To Use RAM Drive," below.

To Load TSRs into High Memory

Many people use memory-resident programs to simplify or improve the way they work. Some are essential, like drivers that let us access certain kinds of hard disks. Others would be hard to live without, like mouse drivers. These memory-resident programs are called TSRs, which is short for Terminate and Stay Resident. The biggest problem with TSRs is that over time we seem to use more and more of them, and pretty soon our system has less and less memory available to run regular programs.

Originally, all DOS programs were limited to using 640KB of memory. This first 640K of memory is referred to as conventional memory, and all programs had to run in this conventional memory, including any TSRs we wanted. As programs became larger, and the desire for more and more TSRs grew, this 640K limit became a problem, and over the years some very ingenious ways have been found to get around this limitation. One of the most readily available on computers based on the 80386 or 80486 chip is the use of the area between 640K and 1024K, known as high DOS memory, or the upper memory area. This 384K area of memory was originally reserved for use by system hardware, such as the video card, the system ROM (and ROM-Basic on IBM PCs), hard disks, network cards, and so on. And it is still used for that. But even after all the various pieces of hardware get done using the memory they need in this region, there is usually a fair amount left over.

In order to get additional memory for use by programs and for data storage, a group of companies (headed by Lotus, Intel, and Microsoft) created the Expanded Memory Specification. This specification defined a way for a special kind of memory, called paged memory, to be created that could be used on XT class computers. This memory required a memory board to be installed in your computer, which came with a special software driver that controlled how this memory was used. If you have an older XT computer and one of these boards, you can skip ahead to "To Use RAM Drive." Modern 80386 and 80486 computers can use extended memory to emulate this kind of memory, using a memory manager.

With the introduction of the IBM PC/AT, and other 80286-based computers, another kind of memory was added. This memory begins just above the upper memory area, starting at 1024K, and is known as extended memory. While conventional DOS programs couldn't use this for much, recently standards have been developed that allow many programs to use this memory. One is the eXtended Memory Specification (XMS), which provides a standard way for programs written to use this memory to address it. The first 64K of this XMS memory is known as the High Memory Area, or HMA. DOS 5 can load most of itself into this area, freeing up some 30+ kilobytes of conventional memory.

Another trick is to move some of those essential TSRs out of regular DOS memory and into the upper memory area. This requires at least a 386 and a memory manager to control the process. If you have DOS 5, you already have the necessary memory manager—the combination of HIMEM.SYS and EMM386.EXE. By using these two programs, you can create the necessary types of memory to give each program the kind of memory it prefers. You can create expanded memory for those programs that can use it, such as Norton Desktop for DOS; XMS memory for those programs that prefer extended memory; high memory to load DOS into; and upper memory blocks (UMBs) to squeeze your TSRs into.

While these two programs come free with DOS 5, and they will do the job, they have some serious limitations. They provide no tools to help you with the process of deciding which TSRs should go into which memory areas, or even which areas of memory are safe to use; and they do not share memory between XMS and expanded memory, so you must decide ahead of time exactly how much of each memory you will need. Even with memory prices being relatively low these days, this is rather wasteful. There are, however, several packages available that overcome these limitations. Two of the best known are the Quarterdeck Expanded Memory Manager–386 (QEMM386), from Quarterdeck, and 386MAX, from Qualitas.

With only the tools included with DOS 5, you can't just run a single utility and have it do the whole job of maximizing your computer's memory. You need to do a lot of the work yourself, but the result can be nearly as much memory recovered as with programs such as QEMM386 or 386MAX, except on complex systems.

● **WARNING**   Before any attempt to maximize memory, make a bootable floppy for your A drive. Copy your current AUTOEXEC.BAT and CONFIG.SYS files onto it. This is an important safety precaution.

To Load TSRs High with DOS 5

1.   Format a system diskette in your A drive. With a 5¼" or 3½" diskette (high density or double density to match the drive), the command is:

> **format a: /s**

2.   Copy your current configuration files onto the bootable diskette you just created in step 1.

> **copy c:\config.sys a:**
> **copy c:\autoexec.bat a:**

3.   Set this diskette aside in a safe place, just in case. If you experience problems booting at any time in this process, you can return to the start by putting the floppy into your A drive and restarting the computer. Then copy the saved configuration files back onto your hard disk.

```
copy a:\config.sys c:\
copy a:\autoexec.bat c:\
```

4. Using any ASCII text editor, for example DOS 5's
   EDIT.COM, edit your CONFIG.SYS file so that the following lines are the first three lines after any hard-disk drivers
   that may be required:

   DEVICE=C:\DOS\HIMEM.SYS
   DEVICE=C:\DOS\EMM386.EXE RAM
   DOS=HIGH,UMB

● **NOTE** This and other examples assume your DOS 5 files are
located in the DOS subdirectory of your C drive. If they are in a
different drive or directory, you will need to modify the examples
accordingly.

5. Examine your CONFIG.SYS file for device drivers that
   can be loaded into high memory. You should not attempt to change device drivers that load disk caches,
   such as the Norton Cache and Microsoft's Smartdrive.
   Generally, if these can be safely loaded into high
   memory, they are smart enough to do so by themselves.
   Modify the line that loads the driver to use DOS 5's
   DEVICEHIGH command. An unmodified line might be:

   DEVICE=C:\DOS\ANSI.SYS

   After being edited, that line would be:

   DEVICEHIGH=C:\DOS\ANSI.SYS

6. Reboot your computer. This will allow the changes you have
   made to take effect. Check to see how much memory is now
   available, using the mem or chkdsk commands. If you have
   freed enough memory, you can stop here, but if you want to
   attempt to free even more, then continue.

7. Using your ASCII text editor again, examine your
   AUTOEXEC.BAT file for TSRs that could be loaded into
   high memory. Here again, many programs, such as the
   Norton Scheduler and Norton SmartCan, are smart
   enough to load themselves into high memory when it is

available. So simply modifying your CONFIG.SYS as you did in step 5 will have caused these programs to load themselves into high DOS memory when you rebooted the computer. For those TSRs that won't automatically load themselves high, DOS 5 provides the LOADHIGH command. An unmodified command line might be:

C:\DOS\SHARE

This command line modified would be:

LOADHIGH C:\DOS\SHARE

8.   After you have made any changes in your AUTOEXEC.BAT file, reboot your computer again so that they will take effect.

9.   Use the DOS 5 mem command to see how much memory is now available and which programs are loaded where:

MEM /C | MORE

10.   If all these changes have not freed enough conventional memory, then you are going to need to invest in a memory manager such as QEMM386 or 386MAX, which will gain you more conventional memory than DOS 5 alone can.

To Use a RAM Drive

A RAM drive is a section of memory that can be treated as if it were another disk drive, just like a floppy disk or hard disk. However, unlike a floppy disk or hard disk, when you reboot your computer everything that was stored on the RAM drive is gone. The advantage to a RAM drive is that, for files that are accessed frequently, it is extremely fast. Norton Desktop for DOS can take advantage of a RAM drive to store its temporary swap files, with a substantial increase in speed. This is available even on XT class computers that don't have extended memory and can't load DOS or other programs into high memory, as long as they have an expanded memory board and an expanded memory manager. If you have at least 512K of expanded memory available, we suggest you create a RAM drive of at least 512K to hold the Norton Desktop for DOS temporary swap files. To create a RAM drive of 512K, using MS-DOS versions 3.3–5.0, insert the following command into your

CONFIG.SYS file *after* the line that invokes your expanded memory manager:

DEVICE=C:\DOS\RAMDRIVE.SYS 512 512 16 /A

This will create a RAM drive of 512K, with a sector size of 512 bytes and a maximum number of directory entries of 16 using expanded memory. The drive letter that this will create will depend on what other drivers you have, how many hard-disk drives you have, and so on, but generally the drive letter will be the first drive letter after your current last hard-disk drive. Assuming you have only a C hard drive, this would be D. You should then run the NDCON-FIG.EXE program to tell Norton Desktop to use this drive for its swap files and temporary files.

Part Two

Configuring the Desktop

The Norton Desktop for DOS is almost infinitely configurable. Most things you can see can be changed to suit the way you work.

BUTTON BAR

The button bar can be omitted by clearing the Display Button Bar check box in the Configure ➤ Button Bar dialog box.

You can change any of the functions on the button bar except F1 (Help) and F10 (opens the pull-down menus). Any command available on the pull-down menus can be assigned to a button.

To Change a Button Command

1. Select Configure ➤ Button Bar.

2. Select the button that you want to change from the list of button bar assignments on the right side of the dialog box.

3. Find the command you want on the list of Available Commands, and double-click on it.

4. Click on the Assign button. The cursor will move to the text box so you can change the name that will appear on the button. The name is limited to six characters.

5. Repeat steps 1 through 4 until you've made all the changes you want. Click on OK when you are finished.

To Reset the Button Bar Assignments

1. Select Configure ➤ Button Bar.

2. In the dialog box, click on the Reset Button. A dialog box will open asking you to confirm that you want to reset the button bar to its default settings. Click on OK.

3. Select OK in the Configure Button Bar dialog box to confirm the change.

CLOCK

A digital clock is displayed on the right side of the Norton Desktop
menu bar. The display can be turned off or displayed in 24-hour
format.

To Change the Clock

1. Select Configure ➤ Clock.

2. In the Configure Clock dialog box, you can change the system time and date by typing in the correct information.

3. Clear the Display Time check box to remove the display
from the menu bar. Check the 24-Hour Time box to have
the time displayed in 24-hour format.

4. Click on OK to confirm your choices.

COMPRESSION

Compressing files can save valuable space on your hard disk.
Several files, or whole directories with subdirectories, can be compressed into a single file. To select and compress files, use the File ➤
Compress command. Options for how the compression is done are
selected under the Configure menu.

To Set Up File Compression

1. Select Configure ➤ Compression.

2.   Make your selections and click on OK when finished.

● OPTIONS–STORAGE METHOD

Automatically Select Best Method   Allows the program to choose whether to implode or shrink files.

Always IMPLODE Files   Forces the program to implode files that take up the smallest amount of space, but is somewhat slower.

Always SHRINK files   Forces the program to use the fastest method of compression, but the resulting files are larger.

● OPTIONS–GENERAL

Store Full Pathnames   Check this box if you want the compressed files to retain their full path in addition to a file name.

Use Temporary Work Directory   If disk space is at a premium and you want to create the compressed file at a location other than where it will be stored, check this box and type in the drive and directory you want to use.

● OPTIONS–TIMESTAMP

Set to Current Date and Time   Assigns the current time and date to the newly created compressed file. This is the default setting. When new material is added to the compressed file, the date will change to the current date and time.

Set to Timestamp of Most Recent File   Assigns the date and time of the newest file to the entire compressed file. If you add a more recent file, the date and time will be changed to match the newest file.

Do Not Change Timestamp   Saves the original date even after file is updated.

● **NOTE**   These options refer to the timestamp of the compressed file. The original files within the compressed file retain their own original timestamps, which will reappear when they are uncompressed.

CONFIRMATION

By default, you are prompted for confirmation when you request certain actions. You can turn off these requests by choosing this command.

To Choose Confirmation Settings

1. Select Configure ➤ Confirmation.

2. Check the operations for which you want a prompt. Clear the other check boxes.

3. Click on OK when you are finished.

DESKTOP LINK

Desktop Link is a utility that allows you to copy and move files from one PC to another without a network. You connect the two computers using a cable and then copy, move, delete, and rename files directly.

To Configure Desktop Link

1. Select Configure ➤ Desktop Link.

2. In the Configure Desktop Link dialog box, there are four drop-down boxes. Choose the options that apply.

3. Click on OK to save your selections when you are finished.

● **OPTIONS–PORT**

Select the communications port you are using to send and receive data. **Auto Detect** will allow Norton Desktop to automatically choose the correct port.

● OPTIONS–BAUD RATE

In the Baud Rate drop-down box, select the rate at which your computer will send data.

● OPTIONS–ERROR CHECKING

Auto   Allows Norton Desktop to select the best method of error checking.

Use Checksum Only   Employs a method by which the ASCII values of all the characters in a block are added together. This number is sent along with the block of data. At the receiving end, the addition is performed again and the results compared. If the numbers are not the same, the block is sent again.

Use CRC Only   This is a slightly slower method that checks for transposition errors as well as for the total characters transmitted.

● OPTIONS–SPEED

Turbo   Sends 4K blocks of data.

Normal   Sends 2K blocks of data.

Slow   Sends 512-byte blocks of data.

Generally, you should leave the speed set at Turbo. If Norton Desktop detects errors, the program will automatically drop the speed.

To Clone Norton Desktop Files

Norton Desktop for DOS must be on both computers for the Desktop Link to work. Not *all* files have to be on both computers, but the Clone option will send the necessary files to another computer.

1.   Connect the two PCs using a serial cable.

2.   At the originating computer, select Configure ➤ Desktop Link.

3.   In the Configure Desktop Link dialog box, click on the Clone button.

4. In the Remote System Port box, select the radio button for the communications port used by the receiving computer.

5. At the receiving computer, go to the DOS prompt for the drive where you want to receive the files. Make a directory called ND and change to that directory.

6. Type the following command:

    MODE COM1:2400,N,8,1,P

    and press Enter. You should see the message Resident portion of mode loaded. Type in

    CTTY COM1:

    If the receiving computer is using COM2, substitute COM2 in the above commands.

7. At the originating (sending) computer, click on the OK button in the Clone dialog box. The necessary files will be transferred.

8. When the file transfer is complete, click on Cancel to leave the Cloning Status box at the sending computer. At the receiving computer, type **ND** and press Enter. The cloned Norton Desktop for DOS will open.

EDITOR

You can choose a text editor other than the default editor provided by Norton Desktop for DOS. The chosen editor will be launched when you choose the Edit command from the File menu, click on Edit in the button bar, or press F4.

To Set the Default Editor

1.   Select Configure ➤ Editor.

2.   In the Configure Editor dialog box, click on the radio button for Built In to select the Norton Desktop for DOS Editor, or External to choose a different editor.

3.   If you choose External, type in the name of the program you want to use. Include the full path unless the program is in your DOS PATH statement or in the Norton Desktop directory. You can use the Browse button to search for the program you want.

4.   When you are finished, click on OK to save your setting.

MOUSE

Mouse speed and sensitivity can be set using the Mouse Options.

To Configure Your Mouse

1.   Select Configure ➤ Video/Mouse.

2.   Choose from the options shown below.

3.   Click on OK to save your settings.

● OPTIONS–DOUBLE-CLICK

Select Slow, Medium, or Fast from the Double-click drop-down list. Fast means that two mouse clicks must be very close together for the program to recognize them as a double-click. Slow means that two clicks can be relatively far apart and the program will still recognize them as a double-click action.

● OPTIONS–SENSITIVITY

Select Default, Low, Medium, or High sensitivity. A high-sensitivity setting will cause the pointer on the screen to move farther with less motion of the mouse on the desktop.

● OPTIONS–ACCELERATION

Choose Default, Low, Medium, or Fast from the Acceleration drop-down list. This setting determines the rate of acceleration for the mouse pointer. At a higher setting, the pointer moves faster the farther it moves on the screen.

● OPTIONS–CHECK BOXES

Graphical Mouse   Select this option to display the mouse cursor as a pointer. Deselect to display the mouse pointer as a rectangle.

Left-handed Mouse   Check this box to make the right mouse button the primary button.

Fast Mouse Reset   When checked, will cause the mouse to reset quickly after any action in which the mouse driver was affected. This option is on by default.

Enter Moves Focus   When this box is checked, using the Enter key causes the highlight to move from place to place in a dialog box. If this box is deselected, using the Enter key will select whatever button is highlighted with the triangular arrowheads (the active command button). Usually, this is the OK button.

NETWORK

Ordinarily, Norton Desktop for DOS will automatically recognize the type of network you are using and adjust itself accordingly. However, if you have more than one network installed, Norton Desktop can recognize only one at a time. You will have to manually configure your connection in order to communicate over the second network.

To Configure Your Network Connection

1. Select Configure ➤ Network.

2. Click on the Network Type prompt button for a list of supported networks. Select the appropriate network type.

3. Click on OK when you are finished.

● **OPTIONS**

Workstation Name   Type in an optional workstation name. This will allow other users to identify your station. This option is not available on Novell networks.

Network Timeout   Sets the length of time Norton Desktop will use to try and establish a connection with another computer on the network. If your network is very busy, you may want to increase the amount of time here.

Enable Network Messages   When checked, will cause network messages to appear in a dialog box. Clear this check box if you want the network to handle network message display.

PASSWORDS

To prevent unauthorized access, password protection is available at several different points. See "Screen Saver/Sleeper" for instructions on passwords to hide your screen. To protect your antivirus configuration, see "Norton AntiVirus" in Part Four.

Passwords can also be assigned to protect menus from being used or changed.

To Assign a Menu Password

1. Select Configure ➤ Password.

2. Type in your password in the New Password text box. The password will appear on the screen as asterisks to prevent it from being seen by others. You will be prompted to type in the password a second time in the Confirm New Password box.

3. Select OK to save your password.

To Change a Menu Password

1. Select Configure ➤ Password.

2. In the Password dialog box, type your current password in the Old Password text box.

3. Key in the new password in the New Password box. Type it in a second time in the Confirm New Password box.

4. Select OK to save the new password.

To Remove a Menu Password

1. Select Configure ➤ Password.

2. Type in your current password in the Old Password text box. Press Enter or use the ↓ key to move the highlight to the New Password text box. Press Enter. A dialog box opens asking if you wish to remove the password. Select Yes.

PREFERENCES

An assortment of options to customize Norton Desktop for DOS is available in the Preferences dialog box. Select the ones that are most useful for you.

To Select Preferences

1. Select Configure ➤ Preferences.

2. Choose the options you want.

3.   Save your selections by clicking on OK, or select Cancel to abandon any changes.

● OPTIONS–GENERAL

Shutdown   Check this box to establish a shutdown routine for when you close Norton Desktop and return to DOS. See "Shutdown Routine," below.

Insert Moves Down   When you are working in a drive window, pressing the insert key will select or deselect the file under the highlight. Check this box if you want the highlight to move down to the next file when you press the insert key.

Shadows on Windows   This box is checked by default. Uncheck it if you want no shadows to appear on open windows.

Scan Floppies for Viruses   Check this box to have Norton AntiVirus scan a floppy disk when you open a window for it. The scan does not occur if you access the floppy disk using a DOS command. The scan is done only when you open a window for the floppy.

Speed Search Preview   When this box is checked, the file listing in the file pane reflects the contents of the highlighted directory. If you uncheck this box, the file listing will not change until you select the directory.

Subdirs with Drag & Drop   Check this box if you want subdirectories included when you use a mouse to copy or move a directory and its files. If this box is not checked, only the directory and the files within that directory will be included in a drag and drop operation.

● OPTIONS–DESKTOP

Style   Using the prompt button, you can choose either the Norton Desktop or the Norton Commander display. For information on the Norton Commander option, see Appendix B.

Keystrokes   Using this option, you can choose whether you want your navigation keys ($\uparrow,\downarrow,\leftarrow,\rightarrow$, Home, End) to act on drive windows or the DOS command line. If you choose Command line first, these keys will act on the DOS command line when the DOS background is on. To navigate in the Norton Desktop window, press the Shift key plus the navigation key.

The reverse is true if you have chosen the Window first option. Then you press the Shift key plus the navigation key to navigate on the command line.

● OPTIONS–DRIVE ICONS

Location   Click on the prompt button to select whether you want the drive icons to be shown on the left, right, or bottom of the screen.

Wide Icons   Check this button if you want a graphic image next to each drive letter. The images, as shown in Figure 2.1, designate each drive as a floppy, hard, or network drive.

Drives   Select the Drives button on the right of the dialog box to choose which drives you want shown as icons. In the Drives dialog box, select the drives you want displayed. Click on OK to save your choices.

● OPTIONS–ADVANCED

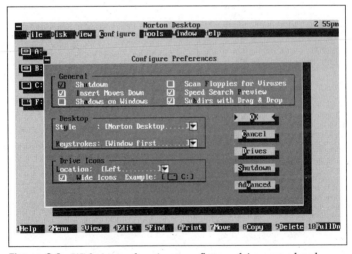

Figure 2.1: Wide icons showing two floppy drives, one hard drive, and a RAM drive

Show Free Disk Space Statistics   Check this box to have a display of free disk space at the top of open drive windows.

Refresh Drive Windows Automatically   Updates lists of files in open drive windows automatically when you return to the desktop.

Refresh Drive Icons Automatically   Updates drive icons after running an external program.

Display Wait... When Busy   If you are not using a mouse, or are using a mouse with the block pointer, checking this box will cause a Wait... message to appear in the upper-left corner of your screen when a long procedure is being performed.

Always Update Master Environment Area   Check this box to allow the use of DOS Interrupt 2E when an external command is executed. This saves a small amount of memory. This check box is dimmed if your software cannot support it.

Update Button Bar to Match Pull-downs   Automatically updates the button bar to match the menu items that have those keys as shortcut keys. This is useful when you have multiple menus with different functions assigned to the same key.

PRINTER

Norton Desktop allows you to set up more than one printer or more than one printing format and save the settings in a configuration file. When you want to change configurations, open the Configure Printer dialog box, click on the file you want to use, and select Close.

To Create a Printer Configuration File

1. Select Configure ➤ Printer

2. In the Configure Printer dialog box, select the Add button. The Configuration Name dialog box opens. Type in a name for the new configuration file. Select OK.

3. Select options and enter the settings you want. Click on OK to save your settings.

4. Your new configuration file will be added to the list in the Configure Printer dialog box. Select the file you want to be active and click on the Close button.

● OPTIONS

Compressed Print   Prints your file in compressed mode.

Wrapped lines   Automatically wraps your text. If this is not checked, you must have a carriage return at the end of each line.

Number lines   Prints a number in left margin for each line of your text.

Printer Type   Click on the prompt button for a list of printer types.

Printer Setup File   Any ASCII file that contains escape sequences needed by the printer. Printer setup files have the extension .NPS.

Margins   Top and bottom margins are measured in rows. Left and right margins are measured in columns.

Page Size   Set total columns and rows on the page.

Line Spacing   Set line spacing (numbers from one through ten are allowed). Space between tabs is measured in columns, with the default being eight.

Header   Select the header type you want. You can choose no header, a single-line header, or a two-line header. Check the Bold Headers box if you want the header to be in boldfaced type.

Output Destination   Specify where the output should be directed.

Data Format   The default setting is ASCII, which uses eight bits to define each character. You can also choose WordStar, which is a format that uses seven bits to define the character and the eighth for control information. Or you can choose EBCDIC, which is used by mainframe computers.

Orientation   If you have specified a PostScript or HP Laser-jet printer, you can choose between portrait and landscape orientation. The landscape orientation prints a page that is wider than it is tall.

To Edit a Printer Configuration File

1.   Select Configure ➤ Printer.

2.   Highlight the file you want to edit in the list of Configuration Files. Select the Edit button.

3.   Make the changes. Select the OK button to save your selections. Select Close in the Configure Printer dialog box.

To Delete or Rename
a Printer Configuration File

1.   Select Configure ➤ Printer.

2.   Highlight the name of the configuration file you want to delete or rename.

3.   Click on the Delete button or the Rename button.

4.   You will be prompted to confirm your choice. Click on OK and then Close.

PULL-DOWN MENUS

The pull-down menus on the desktop can be customized and saved in various configurations to make your work easier. Load and unload menu sets with the click of a button.

To Load a Menu Set

1. Select Configure ➤ Load Pull-downs.

2. In the list of Pull-down Menu Files, highlight the menu set you want to load. You can select the Browse button if the menu set is not in the Norton Desktop directory.

3. Click on OK.

● **NOTE**   The various pull-down menus are saved with the file extension .NDM. By default, these are saved in the Norton Desktop for DOS directory, but you can specify a different location at the time of creation.

To Add a Pull-Down Menu to the Menu Bar

1. Select Configure ➤ Edit Pull-downs.

2. In the Your Menu list on the right of the dialog box, select where you want the new menu to appear on the bar. Highlight a menu name, and your new menu will appear to the right of it on the menu bar. Highlight a command name, and your new menu becomes a submenu of the highlighted item.

3. Click on Custom Menu in the Available Commands list box. Select the Add-> button. The words *Custom Menu* will appear in the Your Menu list. Double-click on Custom Menu, or highlight it and select the Edit button.

4. The Edit Menu dialog box will open.

5. Type in the name you want for the menu in the Menu Name text box. If you are going to use a shortcut key to open this menu, put a caret (^) before the letter you want to highlight.

34   Configuring the Desktop

6.   Click on the Shortcut button to assign a shortcut key combination to the menu. Follow the instructions.

7.   Click on OK in the Edit Pull-down Menu to save your work. At any point, you can click on the Cancel button and start over.

● EXAMPLE

In Figure 2.2, you can see a new menu called *Communications*. On the menu bar, this menu will appear with the first letter *m* in red to remind you that the shortcut key combination of Alt+M will open the menu.

● **NOTE**   When you save your new menu, it will be saved as the standard Norton Desktop long pull-down menu. If you want to save

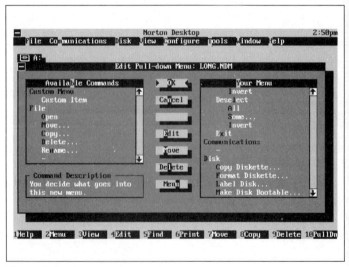

Figure 2.2: Menu bar with new pull-down menu

it as a separate menu set, click on the Menu button in the Edit Pull-down Menu dialog box. Type in a new title and description for the menu. Select Save As and enter the new file name in the File text box. Click on OK.

To Add a Menu Item to a Pull-Down Menu

1. Select Configure ➤ Edit Pull-downs.

2. If the menu you want to edit is not the currently loaded one, you will have to click on the Menu button in the Edit Pull-down Menu dialog box. In the Menu Operations dialog box, click on the Load button. Select the Pull-down Menu File you want and click on OK.

3. In the Your Menu list, highlight the item you want to precede your item.

4. Highlight the item in the Available Commands list and click on the Add-> button. The command will be added to Your Menu. Click on OK to save.

5. To have a shortcut key to call the menu item, highlight the item in the Your Menu window and select Edit. Click on the Shortcut button and follow the instructions.

6. Click on OK when you are finished.

● **NOTE**   When you are assigning a shortcut key, the program will warn you if you attempt to assign a key that is already in use. For example, if you choose the key combination Alt+F, a box will open informing you that this key is already in use to call the File menu. You can select one of the following options:

Try Again   Allows you to assign a different key.

Use Anyway   Results in a duplicate shortcut key assignment. The key will call the item that comes first in the menu.

Cancel   Abandons the attempt to assign a shortcut key.

To Add a Custom Item to a Pull-Down Menu

1. Select Configure ➤ Edit Pull-downs.

2. If the menu you want to edit is not the currently loaded one, you will have to click on the Menu button in the Edit Pull-down Menu dialog box. In the Menu Operations dialog box, click on the Load button. Select the Pull-down Menu File you want and click on OK.

3. In the Your Menu list, highlight the item you want to precede your item.

4. Select Custom Item from the Available Commands list and click on the Add-> button.

5. In the Edit Custom Item dialog box, type in the name of the item as you want it to appear on the menu. Include a caret (^) before the letter you want highlighted as a keyboard shortcut key.

6. In the Command Line box, type the full name for the program you want to execute. If you are not sure of the path, click on the Browse button.

7. To have a shortcut key combination to call the menu item, click on the Shortcut button and follow the instructions.

8. Click on OK to save your new items.

To Edit or Delete a Menu Item from a Pull-Down Menu

1. Select Configure ➤ Load Pull-downs.

2. Highlight the menu set you want to change and click on the OK button.

3. Select Configure ➤ Edit Pull-downs.

4. To Delete an item, highlight it in the Your Menu list and then select the Delete button. The item will be immediately deleted.

5. To edit the item, highlight it in the Your Menu list and select the Edit button. Change the name, change or add a shortcut key, and click on OK when finished.

● **NOTE** To delete an entire menu, open a drive window and go to the directory where the menu file is kept (usually ND). Find the file (it will have the extension .NDM) and delete it.

To Move a Pull-Down Menu or an Item on a Pull-Down Menu

1. Select Configure ➤ Edit Pull-downs.

2. In the Your Menu list, highlight the menu or command you want to move.

3. Click on the Move button. Use the ↑ and ↓ keys to move the item to the position you want. Click on OK when finished.

● **NOTE** If you accidentally delete or modify a menu without intending to, click on the Cancel button and start over. Once you select OK in the Edit Pull-down Menu box, the file is saved in the modified form.

SCREEN

To a great extent, the appearance of your screen can be controlled and customized. Color and display options are covered in this section.

To Configure the Screen

1. Select Configure ➤ Video/Mouse.

2. In the Configure Video/Mouse dialog box, click on the prompt box next to Screen Colors to see a list of available choices. Pick the option you want.

3. Select Display Lines and Display Mode in the same manner.

4. Click on OK to save your choices when finished.

● OPTIONS

Screen Colors Choose the display option you want. Or you can select Custom Colors to design your own color scheme. See "To Customize Colors," below.

Display Lines If you have a VGA or EGA monitor, you can change the number of lines displayed on the screen. Otherwise, Norton Desktop for DOS sets the display to match the setting of your screen.

Display Mode You can choose from Standard, Some Graphical Controls, or All Graphical Controls. Depending on which one you choose, there will be differences in how check boxes, drive and file icons, and other graphical elements appear on your screen.

Zooming Boxes With this box checked, dialog boxes will appear to zoom open rather than appear on the screen all at once. With a fast computer, you may not be able to tell the difference. This box is checked by default.

Solid Background This box is checked by default except when using Monochrome. Clear the check if you prefer the textured background.

Button Arrows Clear this box to remove the triangular arrowheads from the active command button. In some color settings, the active command button displays in a different color so the arrowheads are not necessary. The arrowheads cannot be removed in the Monochrome, Black and White, or Greyscale (Laptop) settings.

Block Cursor Check this box to have the cursor appear on the screen as a rectangle instead of an underscore.

To Customize Colors

1. Select Configure ➤ Video/Mouse.

2. Select Custom Colors or any other color scheme from the drop-down list under Screen Colors. Click on the Customize Colors button.

3. The Customize Colors dialog box opens, as shown in Figure 2.3. On the left side is a list of all the elements on the desktop that can be changed. As you scroll through them, a sample window on the right shows the selected element and its current color scheme. Select the element you want to change.

4. Click on the Color button or press Enter. The Colors dialog box opens. As shown in Figure 2.4, the title bar at the top shows the name of the element. Below that is a sample window. The triangles under the color bars indicate the current color selections and can be moved using the mouse or the → and ← keys.

5. When you have the color combination you want, click on the OK button. The Default button in this dialog box can be used to return the selected element to its default colors.

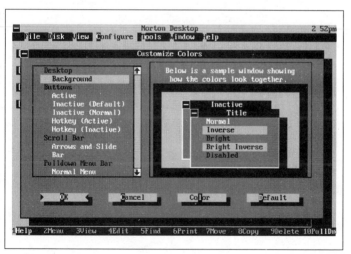

Figure 2.3: The Customize colors dialog box

Figure 2.4: The Colors dialog box

6. Repeat the above steps until all the desktop elements have been customized. Click on OK to save your color settings. The Default button in the Customize Colors dialog box can be used to return *all* the colors on the desktop to their default settings.

To Change the Screen Background

In addition to being able to select a solid or textured background as described above, you can also run the desktop with a DOS background. This gives you not only the DOS history on screen but a command line prompt.

1. Select View ➤ DOS Background, or enter Ctrl+O from the keyboard.

2. The DOS background will remain in place until you pull down the menu and remove the check mark.

SCREEN SAVER/SLEEPER

To configure the Screen Saver/Sleeper, it must be installed. If it was not part of the original installation, you must run the Install program and select Scheduler/Screen Saver. For help, see Part One.

Once installed, Screen Saver/Sleeper will be available only in Norton Desktop for DOS unless you make it into a screen saver for all your DOS programs. To do that, install it as a startup program (see "Startup Programs" below).

To Configure Screen Saver/Sleeper

1. Select Configure ➤ Screen Saver.

2. Select the Screen Saver Type from the drop-down list in the dialog box. To preview the screen saver before committing yourself, click on the Test button. The screen saver pattern will appear. Return to the dialog box by pressing any key or by moving the mouse.

3. From the Screen Blank Delay drop-down list, select the amount of time you want the program to wait before starting the screen saver pattern. For example, if you select 15 minutes, your computer must be inactive for 15 minutes before the screen saver comes on.

4. Click on the radio buttons to select Sleep Now and Never Sleep corners. When you move the mouse pointer to the Sleep Now corner, the screen saver becomes active even if the Screen Blank Delay is set to Off. When you move the mouse pointer to the Never Sleep corner, the Screen Saver will not become active during this session of Norton Desktop for DOS unless you move the pointer to the Sleep Now corner.

5. Check the Use Password box if you want the program to require a password in order to restore your work screen. Click on the Password button and type in the password. Note that this only protects your current screen from being seen. Your files can still be accessed by rebooting the computer.

6.   Check the Wake on Mouse Movement if you want the screen saver to clear away when the mouse is moved. If this box is not checked, a keystroke is required to return to the screen.

7.   Click on the Hotkey button to assign a hotkey combination that will instantly turn on the screen saver. The default hot key is Ctrl+Alt+Z, but you can choose any character plus any combination of the four special keys. Click on OK to save your choice.

8.   When you have made your Screen Saver choices, click the OK button.

● **NOTE**   If you select Message or .PCX file as your Screen Saver Type, you will need to click on the Configure button and provide additional information.

To have a message display, click on Configure and then type in a message of up to 34 characters. Click on OK twice. Your message will appear on the screen when Screen Saver is active.

To have a .PCX file display, click on the Configure button, then type in the name of the .PCX file, including the path. Select OK twice.

To Disable Screen Saver/Sleeper

The Screen Saver should be turned off when you use a telecommunications program or any other application that should not be interrupted.

- Select Configure ➤ Screen Saver. In the Screen Blank Delay drop-down list, select Off. Select OK. This will disable the screen saver, except that the Sleep Now Corner will still be available.

- To turn off the Screen Saver/Sleeper function completely, select Configure ➤ Startup Programs. Remove the check mark from in front of Start Scheduler/Screen Saver either by double-clicking or by using the space bar. Click on the Save button. Reboot your computer to put the change into effect. Screen Save/Sleeper will now be available only when Norton Desktop is active on the screen.

SAVE CONFIGURATION

Most configuration changes are saved and used for future sessions. However, the appearance of your desktop needs to be specifically saved to have it reappear in the same form the next time you start Norton Desktop for DOS.

To Save Your Desktop Configuration

1. Arrange the desktop and settings the way you want them for future Norton Desktop for DOS sessions.

2. Select Configure ➤ Save Configuration.

SHUTDOWN ROUTINE

You can specify a number of operations for Norton Desktop for DOS to perform whenever you leave the program and return to DOS. These tasks can include sending mail, backing up disks, and other housekeeping operations.

To Define a Shutdown Routine

1. Select Configure ➤ Preferences. In the Configure Preferences dialog box, check the Shutdown check box.

2. Click on the Shutdown command button. The Shutdown dialog box opens.

3. In the Upon Exiting ND drop-down list, you select what you want to happen when you exit Norton Desktop:

> **Exit to DOS** simply returns you to a DOS prompt.
> **Secure Computer** locks the computer until a password is supplied. If you choose this option, you must select the Password command button and enter a password.
> **Reboot** causes your computer to restart so that all memory is cleared.

4. In the Before Shutting Down box, select the operations you want performed *before* you exit from Norton Desktop.

5. Click on the Drives button to select the drives you want checked in the Shutdown routine.

6. Click on OK. To use the Shutdown routine, you must click on the Shutdown command button when exiting Norton Desktop, as shown in Figure 2.5. If you select the Exit button, the Shutdown routine does not run.

Figure 2.5: To run the Shutdown routine, you must select Shutdown in the Exit dialog box.

● OPTIONS–SHUTDOWN

Backup Disks   Select this to run Norton Backup. When this box is checked, the drop-down list becomes active and you can choose a customized .SET file. For more information on Norton Backup, see "Norton Backup" in Part Four.

Send/Receive Mail   If you have MCI mail, this option will automatically send messages in your OUT folder and copy new messages into your IN folder. See "Norton Mail" in Part Four for more information.

Check Disks   Norton Disk Doctor runs tests on your partition table, file allocation table, boot record, and directory structure and looks for lost clusters. Additional information can be found in "Norton Disk Doctor" in Part Four.

Scan Disk for Viruses   Runs Norton AntiVirus. See "Norton AntiVirus" in Part Four.

Optimize Disks   Your hard disks are defragmented using Speed Disk. See "Speed Disk" in Part Four.

Image Disk Info   A new Image file is created for each hard drive. For information on Image, see "Image" in Part Five.

Logout from Network   Disconnects your computer from the network.

STARTUP PROGRAMS

You can configure a selection of programs as Startup Programs. That is, the programs install themselves every time you turn on your computer.

To Select Startup Programs

1.   Select Configure ➤ Startup Programs.

2.   In the Startup Programs dialog box, select the programs you want loaded every time you start the computer. Double-click on the program or move the highlight to the

program name and press the spacebar. A check mark
before the program name means it is selected.

3. Depending on how you select the program, the configuration options will open or you will have to select
the Configure button. Configure will be dimmed if
there are no options to select.

4. Below the list of startup programs, a status line indicates
the available memory and the amount used. As you select
programs, the amount of memory available is reduced.

5. Click on the Edit button for direct access to your
AUTOEXEC.BAT and CONFIG.SYS files. Using the
Editing Startup Files dialog box, you can highlight lines
and move them by clicking on the Move button. You can
also highlight lines and delete them by selecting the
delete button. It is not advisable to change your startup
files without saving copies in another location.

6. You can check Add Directory to Path and Set ND
Environment Variable for any highlighted program,
whether or not it is selected. Use the Edit button to see
the effect your changes will have on your startup files.

7. When you have made your choices, select Save.

● OPTIONS–STARTUP PROGRAMS

Diagnose Disk Problems   Norton Disk Doctor will check
your file allocation table, partition table, file and directory
structure, boot record, and lost clusters. For more information,
see "Norton Disk Doctor" in Part Four.

Save Disk Format Data   Runs the Image program, which
records the system information on your hard disk. This can
make it possible to recover from an accidental format or other
disaster. For information on Image, see "Image" in Part Five.

Scan Drives for Viruses   Instructs Norton AntiVirus to scan
all or selected drives for viruses. See "Norton AntiVirus" in Part
Four for more information.

Start Desktop   Select this option and Norton Desktop for DOS will automatically start when you turn on your computer.

Start SmartCan   Works with Unerase to ensure that deleted files can be recovered with 100 percent reliability. For more information, see "SmartCan" in Part Five.

Start Scheduler/Screen Saver   Loads the memory-resident program necessary to run Scheduler (see "Scheduler" in Part Four and "Screen Saver/Sleeper," above).

Start Norton Cache   Loads the memory-resident program that uses RAM to speed up hard-disk reading operations. For information on how to configure Norton Cache, see "Norton Cache" in Part Five.

Start Norton AntiVirus   Installs a driver to allow Norton AntiVirus to scan for viruses in files as they are being used. See "Norton AntiVirus" in Part Four for information on how to configure Norton AntiVirus.

Part Three

Managing Files

ASSOCIATING A FILE

When you associate a file name extension with an application, you can then launch any file with that extension and have the associated program automatically open. Norton Desktop for DOS even lets you add custom command line options as you launch the program, depending on the extension of the file that initiated the launching. This gives Norton Desktop for DOS the ease of program association that Windows has, and that is totally lacking in plain DOS. Further, Norton Desktop for DOS makes it easy to add, change, or delete associations through the use of dialog boxes.

To Add an Association

1. Choose File ➤ Associate.

2. Select Add to bring up the Add Association dialog box. (Optionally, if you launch a file that does not already have an association, you will be offered the choice to add one. If you choose to add the association, the Add Association dialog box will open.)

3. Type the application program's full path name (including extension) in the Program box. Optionally, use the Browse button to look for the file.

4. In the Extension box, type the extension to associate with this program. Do not include the period (.) in the extension.

5. The Optional Command Line box shows ^.^. This will automatically expand to the file name when the associated file is opened from anywhere in Norton Desktop for DOS. You can add any additional command line parameters you want here.

6. Select OK. This returns you to the Associate dialog box. Select OK again to confirm the addition.

● EXAMPLE

Norton Desktop for DOS already knows about some associations. For example, it knows that files that end with the extension .WQ1 are QuattroPro files. But if you want, you can add the extension .WQ! as an association to QuattroPro, since this is the extension with which QuattroPro saves files when it uses SQZ! file compression.

To Change an Association

1. Choose File ➤ Associate.
2. Select the association to change from the List Box.
3. Select Edit to bring up the Edit Association dialog box.
4. Make the changes you want by typing over the existing entries or adding to the Optional Command Line box.
5. Select OK. This returns you to the Associate dialog box. Select OK again to confirm your change.

To Delete an Association

1. Choose File ➤ Associate.
2. Select the association to delete from the List Box.
3. Select Delete. The highlighted association is immediately deleted.
4. Select OK to confirm the deletion, or Cancel to abandon any changes.

To Specify Custom Startup Commands

1. Choose File ➤ Associate.
2. Select Add to add a new association, or Edit to change an existing one.
3. Press Alt+T or click in the Optional Command Line box, and type in the command line parameters to use when the program is run. This can be any command line parameter that the program accepts. For example, it can be the name

of a macro that you want to run every time you start this
program with this extension.

4.   Select OK to confirm. Select OK again in the Associate
dialog box.

● **NOTES**   Norton Desktop for DOS will not allow wildcards in
associated extensions. You must explicitly specify each extension
you wish to associate with a given program.

A particular extension can only be associated with a single program, but any program can have as many extensions associated
with it as is needed.

See Also   Launching Files

ATTRIBUTES

Files can have one of four attributes—Hidden, System, Read Only,
or Archive. Hidden files are not normally visible, but they can be
seen in Norton Desktop for DOS if desired. System files are also
hidden from normal view. This attribute is used by DOS to designate the files it uses during the initial boot sequence. Read Only
files can be viewed with the Viewer or copied but cannot be edited,
changed, or deleted. The Archive attribute designates whether a file
has been backed up since the last time it was modified.

To Change a File's Attributes

1.   Choose File ➤ Properties.

2.   Type in the file name (wildcards OK), or use the Browse
box to select the file(s).

3.   In the Attributes box click on the check boxes of the attributes you want set.

4.   Select OK to confirm the operation, or Cancel to abort
without change.

● **NOTE** If a drive window is open, highlight the files to change first, then select Properties from the File menu.

COMPRESS

Compress lets you reduce the size of a file so that it takes less disk space, or combine a group of files into a single archive file.

To Compress Files

1. Choose File ➤ Compress. The Compress dialog box will open.

2. Enter into the Compress text box the file name of the file to be compressed. Use wildcards to compress a group of files. If you have a drive window open with files or subdirectories selected, the Compress text box will be missing and the number of files selected will be shown.

3. Key a file name for the compressed file in the To text box. You do not need to include an extension; Norton Desktop for DOS will automatically assume a .ZIP extension.

4. Enter an encryption password and confirm it, if you want the file to be password protected.

5. Check the Include Subdirectories box if you want to include all subdirectories of the selected directory in the compressed file.

6. Check the Delete Files Afterwards box if you want Norton Desktop to delete the files that have been compressed after the compressed file has been created.

7. Select Options to override any of the default compression options. For a discussion of the options available, see "Compression" in Part Two.

8. Select OK to begin the compression, or Cancel to abort the operation.

To Uncompress a File

1.   Select the compressed file in a drive window and press
Enter or double-click on it. Or choose Window ➤ Open
Window. The Open Window dialog box will open. Under
Window Type, choose Compressed File, then enter the
compressed file you want by typing the name in the Drive
text box or by using the Browse button to search for it.

2.   A drive window showing all the files within the compressed
file will open.

3.   To uncompress one or more files, select the files to be uncompressed and then copy or move them to another drive
or directory. The files will be uncompressed as the move
or copy is executed.

To View the Contents of a Compressed File

1.   Double-click on the compressed file in a drive window, or
press Enter while the file is highlighted. Or choose Window ➤ Open Window and select the Compressed File
radio button. Select Browse to open the Browse for compressed file dialog box. Select OK to open a compressed
file window, or Cancel to cancel the operation.

2.   With the compressed file window open, you can move,
copy, or delete the files within the archive, using the same
methods as with a regular drive window. You cannot,
however, view, edit, or print the files within the compressed file without first uncompressing them.

COPY

Copy lets you copy a single file or whole subdirectories. It can be
used from the desktop, or when in the drive windows.

To Copy a File or Files

1. Choose File ➤ Copy, or press the F8 key.

2. The Copy dialog box opens. In the Copy text box type in the file name (wildcards OK) of the file you want to copy.

3. The To box is a combination box. Either type in the destination or select from the list of recent destinations. Optionally, click on the Select button to open up a Browse box and choose the destination.

4. Select OK to begin the copy operation, or Cancel to cancel it.

● **SHORTCUT**   From an open drive window, select the files or subdirectories you want to copy and then drag them to the Copy button on the button bar at the bottom of the desktop, to a drive icon on the side of the desktop, or to the desired directory in the Tree Pane of any open drive window.

● **NOTES**   If a subdirectory is being copied, Copy will create that subdirectory at the destination if it is not already there.

To copy subdirectories of the source directory, check the Include Subdirectories box in the Copy dialog box.

DELETE

File Delete lets you delete a single file or whole subdirectories.

To Delete a File or Files

1. Select File ➤ Delete or press the F9 key.

2. The Delete dialog box opens. Type in the file name of the file in the Delete text box. Optionally, open up a Browse box and choose the file(s) to delete.

3.   Select OK to begin the delete operation, or Cancel to cancel it.

● **SHORTCUT**   Select the files or subdirectories in a drive window and drag them to the Delete button on the button bar at the bottom of the desktop.

● **NOTE**   To delete subdirectories of the selected directory, check the Include Subdirectories box in the Delete dialog box.

EDITING FILES

Files can be edited using either the default editor, called the Norton Desktop Editor, or another editor of your choice. To select another editor, see "Editor" in Part Two.

FILE OPERATIONS

The Norton Desktop Editor makes it easy to open multiple files and cut and paste text between those files, insert one file into another, print the file, or save it with a new name.

To Edit a File

1.   If the Norton Desktop Editor isn't yet open, choose File ➤ Edit, press the F4 key, or select Edit from the button bar. If a file is highlighted in a drive window, the Editor will load that file when it opens. If the editor is already open, choose File ➤ Open to open an existing file. The Browse for Edit dialog box will open. Choosing File ➤ New will open a new, untitled file window, bypassing steps 2 and 3.

2.   Type in the name of the file to edit in the File box. Optionally, use the browse features to find and select the file.

3.   Select OK to begin editing the file, or Cancel to abort the operation.

● **SHORTCUT**   Select a file to edit in a drive window and drag it to the Edit button on the button bar at the bottom of the desktop.

● **NOTES**   While the Norton Desktop Editor can have multiple files open simultaneously, only a single file may be selected to edit at a time. Also, the Norton Desktop Editor is a plain ASCII text editor and can only be used on ASCII files, such as batch files.

To Close a File

1.   Choose File ➤ Close. If the file has not changed since the last time it was saved, it will close.

2.   If the file has changed since the last time it was saved, a Caution box will open offering you the chance to save your changes before closing. Choose Yes to save the file and then close it, No to close the file without saving, and Cancel to return to the edit mode without saving the current changes.

To Save a File

1.   Choose File ➤ Save to save the file, or press Ctrl+S. The file is saved, but no backup file is created.

2.   If the file is a new file, or if you choose File ➤ Save As, the Save As dialog box opens. Type the new file name into the File text box, and select the drive and subdirectory for the file, using the browse options. Select OK to save the file, or Cancel to return to the edit screen without saving.

To Insert One File into Another

1.   Open the primary file using File ➤ Open, or if the file is already open, bring its window to the front by choosing Windows, and select it.

2. Position the cursor at the point you want the file to be inserted.

3. Choose File ➤ Insert or press Ctrl+E, and the File to Insert dialog box will open. Select the file to insert.

4. Choose OK to insert the selected file at the cursor, or Cancel to cancel the operation, returning to the edit window.

To Print a File

1. Open the file to be printed, or if it is already open, select its window.

2. Choose File ➤ Print to print the file with the currently selected printer options.

3. Choose File ➤ Print Setup to open the Configure Printer dialog box. See "Printer" in Part Two for details on printer configuration.

EDITING OPERATIONS

While the Norton Desktop Editor is by no means a full-featured word processor, it can be used to do basic cut and paste operations, as well as search and replace.

To Cut, Copy, and Paste Text

1. Select the text to cut or copy using either the mouse or Shift plus the cursor movement keys. Choose Edit ➤ Select All to select all the text in the current file.

2. Choose Edit ➤ Cut (Ctrl+X) to delete the selected text and copy it to the paste buffer, or Edit ➤ Copy (Ctrl+C) to copy it to the paste buffer without deleting it.

3. Move the cursor to the position to insert the text. If you want to place it in another file, open that file or switch to its window.

4. Choose Edit ➤ Paste (Ctrl+V) to paste the contents of the paste buffer at the cursor.

To Delete Text

1. Select the text to delete using either the mouse or Shift plus the cursor movement keys.

2. Choose Edit ➤ Clear or press the Del key.

To Search for Text

1. Choose Search ➤ Find (Ctrl+F) to open the Find dialog box.

2. Type in the text to find in the Find What text box.

3. Check the Match Case box if you want the search to be case sensitive.

4. Choose the Forward or Backward radio buttons to control the search direction.

5. Select Find Next to search for the text, or Cancel to return to the edit window.

To Search and Replace Text

1. Choose Search ➤ Replace (Ctrl+R) to open the Replace dialog box.

2. Type in the text to find in the Find What text box.

3. In the Replace With text box, type in the text with which to replace the found text.

4. Check the Match Case box if you want the search to be case sensitive.

5. Select Find Next to search for the text, Replace to replace it and move to the next occurrence, or Cancel to return to the edit window.

To Reformat Text

1. Choose Options ➤ Page Width to open the Page Width dialog box.

2.   Type in the desired page width (80 columns is the default).

3.   Select OK to set the new page width, or Cancel to keep the old one.

● **NOTE**   Steps 4 and 5 are necessary only if the file contains extra, manually entered carriage returns. This is unlikely unless the file was created with Word Wrap off.

4.   Select the portion of the file to be reformatted. If no text is selected, the reformat will be from the cursor position up to the first blank line.

5.   Choose Edit ➤ Reformat to reformat the selected text to the desired line width.

FIND/SUPERFIND

When you select File ➤ Find, the SuperFind window opens. Super-Find can search for a specific file or for files that match a specific pattern, such as all files with the letters *MEMO* in their file names, or all files with a .TXT extension. SuperFind can also perform a text search for files that contain text you are looking for.

Using the combination boxes and the More button, your search can be defined in a number of ways: according to the file name, extension, location on the drive, and even the time of day the file was created.

To Search for a File

1.   Select File ➤ Find. Key in the name of the file including any extension in the Find Files box, or click on the arrow next to the box to see the default choices.

2.   In the Where box, key in the path to be searched or select an option from the combination box.

3.   Click on the Find button. The Directory line at the bottom of the dialog box shows the progress of the search. Files matching the criteria in the Find Files box will appear in a window below the dialog box. Each subsequent search will produce a new window on top of the previous one.

To Search for Text in a File

1.   Key in the range of files and areas to be searched in the Find Files and Where boxes. If you want to search all files, click the prompt button on the Find Files combination box and select All Files.

2.   In the With Text box, key in the text string that you want to find. The total amount of text, including spaces, must be no more than 30 characters. For an exact match, including upper- and lowercase letters, select Options ➤ Match Upper/Lowercase. Your four most recent text searches can be seen by clicking on the With Text prompt button.

3.   When you have filled in all the search parameters, click the Find button.

● **OPTIONS–FIND FILES BOX**

All Files   Same as the *.* file specification.

All Files Except Programs   Searches for all files except those with .EXE, .COM, .BTM, and .BAT extensions.

Database Files   Searches for all dBASE-compatible files (.DB?) and all Q&A data files (.DTF)

Documents   Finds all .DOC, .TXT, and .WRI files.

Programs   Finds files with program extensions: .EXE, .COM, .BTM, and .BAT.

Spreadsheet Files   Finds all Lotus (.WK?), Quattro (.WQ?), and Excel (.XLS) worksheets.

● **NOTES**   You can use the standard DOS wildcards * and ? to specify files in the Find Files box, plus the pipe character (|), which represents one or zero characters.

You can search for several types of files at once by separating each file specification with a delimiter character: comma(,), semicolon(;), plus sign (+), or space.

To exclude a file type from your search, precede it with a minus sign (−).

● EXAMPLES

| | |.* searches for all file names with three or fewer characters.

COR*.* searches for all file names beginning with the characters *COR*.

.TXT,.BMP searches for .TXT and .BMP files.

. −.WPF searches for all files except those with the .WPF extension.

● OPTIONS–WHERE BOX

Current Drive Only

All Drives

All Drives Except Floppies

Current Dir and Subdir

Current Directory Only

Floppy Drives Only

Local Hard Drives Only

Network Drives Only

Path

● OPTIONS–MORE >> BUTTON

This button opens up the SuperFind window, as shown in Figure 3.1, so you can define your choices even further. With these options you can set the following:

Attributes are the five tri-state boxes on the lower-right side of the screen. They are three-way toggles. A blank check box means the program will search only for files with that attribute bit turned off. An *X* in the box means files must have this bit on for SuperFind to recognize them. A grayed box means the setting of the bit is ignored.

Date, Time, and **Size** boxes are set to Ignore by default. Click on any of the prompt buttons to see the choices available. When you select one of these options, one or more text boxes pop up for you to complete.

To Set Up Search Sets

The default file and location search sets can be modified or deleted and new sets can be added up to a total of 16 file sets and 16 location sets.

1. Select Options ➤ Search Sets to see the Search Sets window, shown in Figure 3.2

2. Click on either the File Sets or Location Sets button.

3. To add a search set, click on Add. Key in the name of the set and the definition in the text boxes. Wildcards and delimiters, as defined above, can be used. Click on OK to

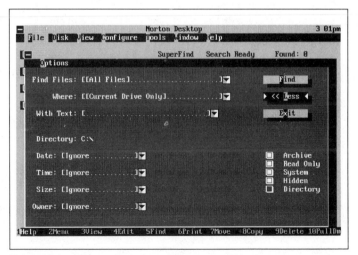

Figure 3.1: The expanded SuperFind window

Figure 3.2: The Search Sets window

confirm the addition. The new set will be added to the
Search Sets list.

4. To edit or delete a set, highlight the set with the mouse
and click on Edit or Delete. Click on OK to confirm the
change.

● **WARNING** Use the Delete button with caution. The deletion
will be made immediately without a warning notice. If you press
Delete in error, click on the Cancel button to save the deleted item.

To Create a Batch File from a File List

1. After SuperFind has found your file or files, select Options
➤ Create Batch from the menu bar.

2. Key in a name for the batch file in the Save As box. Select
the Browse button to browse for a directory in which to
place the batch file.

3. Key in any batch instructions you want in the Insert Before Filename and Append After Filename text boxes. Select options that you want to include. Choose Launch to test the batch file in DOS. An error in the batch file will cause it to abort. To find the source of the error, check the Pause After Each Command box to step through the batch.

4. Select OK to save the batch file.

● **OPTIONS–BATCH FILES**

Full Path Inserts the full path name for each file in the batch file if files in the batch file are located in different directories. The default is On.

Spaces Around Filename Automatically enters blank spaces before and after the file name on each command line of the batch file. The default is On.

Call Each Command Inserts the batch language CALL command at the beginning of each line of the batch file.

Pause After Each Command Inserts a pause after each operation in the batch file. When launching a batch file, you can then examine each command as it is executed.

LAUNCHING FILES

You can open a file and its associated application from virtually anywhere in Norton Desktop for DOS. If you launch an application, it executes. If you open a document file, its associated application executes and the file opens. If the file is not associated with an application, Norton Desktop for DOS prompts you to create an association. For more information about associations and how to create and customize them, see "Associating a File" in this section.

To Launch a File from the File Pane

1. Select Window ➤ Open drive window, or double-click on the appropriate drive icon.

2. Double-click on the file name in the drive window, or highlight it with the cursor movement keys and then press the Enter key.

To Launch a File from the DOS Command Line

1. If the DOS Background is not currently turned on, press Ctrl+O, or select DOS Background from the View menu.

2. Key in the command to start the program on the DOS command line at the bottom of the desktop, including any command line parameters.

To Launch a File from the Run Dialog Box

1. Choose File ➤ Run or press Ctrl+R.

2. The Run dialog box opens. Key in the DOS command to execute, or use the browse box to find the program to execute. Press Ctrl+↓ to drop down a list of the last 10 commands executed.

3. Select Pause on return if you want to stay at the DOS prompt following execution of the command, or clear the check box if you want to return directly to the desktop following execution of the command.

4. Select OK to execute the command.

● **NOTE** Pause on return is disabled if the View ➤ DOS Background is on.

See Also Associating a File

MAKE DIRECTORY

To organize your files into logical groups and prevent directories from becoming too large, you can make new subdirectories to keep track of your files.

To Make a New Directory

1. Choose File ➤ Make Directory.

2. The Make Directory dialog box opens. Key in the name, including the path, of the directory you wish to create in the New Directory text box.

3. Click on Select >> to see a directory tree of the current drive. Click on the directory where you want to create a new subdirectory. Other drives can be selected in the Drive drop-down box.

4. Select OK to make the directory, or Cancel to return.

MOVE

Norton Desktop for DOS makes it easy to move files or entire directories, including subdirectories, to another location, even across drives.

To Move a File

1. Select File ➤ Move, or press F7.

2. In the Move text box, type in the file name, including the path of the file to be moved.

3. In the To text box, type in the destination of the file, including the path, or choose Select >> to open up a browse box where you can select the destination.

4. Check the Include Subdirectories box to include any subdirectories in the move.

5. Select OK to move the files, or Cancel to abort the operation.

● **SHORTCUT**   From an open drive window, select the files or subdirectories you want to move, and then drag them to the Move button on the button bar at the bottom of the desktop, or press the F7 key.

OPENING FILES

When you select File ➤ Open, the file that is highlighted in the File Pane of a drive window opens. If the file has no association, you will be prompted to create one.

See Also   Associating a File

PRINTING FILES

Selecting and configuring a printer are covered in "Printer" in Part Two.

To Print a File

1. Select File ➤ Print, or press F6.

2. When the Browse for Print dialog box opens, type in the name of the file in the File text box and select OK to start printing.

If you are not sure of the file name, use the Directories and Files lists to find the file you want. Double-click on the file name and printing will start.

You can also highlight the file you want in a drive window and press F6.

PROPERTIES

The properties of a file include its date, time, and DOS-assigned attributes. These properties can be changed using the File ➤ Properties command.

To Change File Properties

1. Highlight a file in a drive window.

2. Select File ➤ Properties. The Properties dialog box opens, as shown in Figure 3.3.

3. Using the Description line, you can add a description of the file up to 40 characters long.

4. Make any desired changes to the tri-state boxes in At-tributes. See "Attributes" in this section for information on attributes.

5. To change the Timestamp, select the File Date or File Time check boxes and type in the change.

6. Check the Include Subdirectories box to change the proper-ties of files in subdirectories of the selected directory.

7. Select OK to save your changes.

70   Managing Files

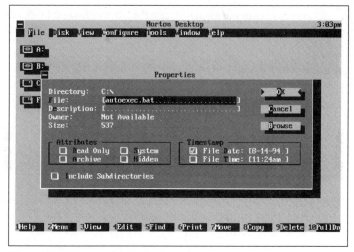

Figure 3.3: Properties dialog box

PRUNE AND GRAFT

The Prune and Graft command enables you to move entire directories and subdirectories from one part of the tree structure to another.

To Prune and Graft a Directory

1. Open the drive window containing the directory you want to move. The View ➤ Tree Pane must be toggled On.
2. Highlight the directory.
3. Select Disk ➤ Prune & Graft.
4. Use ↑ or ↓ to move the directory to its new position. Press Enter to confirm the new position, or Esc to cancel the move.

● **NOTE**   Prune & Graft works only within the same drive. Use the Move command to shift directories between drives.

RENAME

Using the Rename command, you can rename a file, directory, or subdirectory. You can highlight the item to be renamed or fill in the information directly.

To Use Rename

1. Select File ➤ Rename.

2. The name of the file or directory last highlighted will appear in the Rename dialog box. In the To text box, type in the new name.

3. Select OK to save the change, or Cancel to abandon the change.

RUN

If you are running with a DOS background, directions can be given to DOS directly at the command line at the bottom of the screen. If you are running with the default Norton Desktop for DOS background, you will need to use the Run command.

See "To Launch a File from the Run Dialog Box," in *Launching Files*, above.

SELECT AND DESELECT

You can select files in drive windows using the mouse and keyboard. However, for large numbers of files, it's easier to use the Select and Deselect commands in the File menu.

Using Select and Deselect

1. To select files in a file pane, click on File ➤ Select. You can then choose All, Some, or Invert.

All will cause every file shown in the file pane to be marked.

Some will open a dialog box where you can type in the specifications for files you want. Wildcard designations can be used. Or you can choose from a list of recent selections by clicking on the prompt button next to the File text box.

Invert will reverse the previous selection. That is, selected files will become unselected and unselected files will become selected.

2. To deselect files in a pane, choose File ➤ Deselect. The above three choices are available here also.

VIEWING FILES

The Viewer in Norton Desktop for DOS lets you look at the contents of files without having to open an application. Files can be viewed by opening the view pane or by opening the full-screen Viewer.

To View a File

1. Open a drive window and highlight the file you want to view.

2. Select View ➤ View Pane. To change from the View Pane to full-screen mode, click on the View button in the button bar or select File ➤ View.

3. Close the View Pane by selecting View ➤ View Pane again. Close the full-screen viewer by selecting File ➤ Exit or entering Alt+X from the keyboard.

To Change the Viewer Type

Viewers are automatically assigned by Norton Desktop for DOS. A file association does not need to exist. You can change the viewer to another display type.

1. If you are in the Desktop with a View Pane only, select View ➤ Viewer ➤ Change Viewer. If you are in the full-screen Viewer, select View ➤ Change Viewer.

2. Select the Viewer type you want. If the type you select is incompatible, you will get the error message:

Error Viewing File

Incorrect viewer type or file damaged.

Select OK to remove this message. All files can be viewed in ASCII and Hex format.

To Go to a Specific Location in a File

In any file, but particularly a database or spreadsheet file, you may want to go to a particular location that is not identifiable as text.

1. If you are looking at the file in the View Pane, select View ➤ Viewer ➤ Go To. If you are in the full-screen Viewer, select Search ➤ Go To.

2. Depending on the type of file you are viewing, type in the location you want:

Database file   Type the record number.

Spreadsheet file   Type the cell number with the column number first, followed by the row number (A6, H14, and so on).

Hexadecimal format   Type in the hex offset number.

Other file types   Type in the line number.

3. Click on OK to start.

To Search for Text in the Viewer

1. If you are looking at the file in the View Pane, select View ➤ Viewer ➤ Find. If you are in the full-screen Viewer, select Search ➤ Find.

2. In the Search Text text box, type in the word or phrase you want to find.

3. Choose from the search options:

Ignore Case   Check this box if you want capitalization to be ignored.

Multiple Finds   Allows for a repetitive search. After the first find, the dialog box will remain open. Click on Find to go to the next occurrence.

Forward   Searches from the current position forward toward the end of the file.

Backward   Searches from the current position back toward the beginning of the file.

4. Click on Find to begin the search.

After you close the dialog box, you can search again for the same work or phrase by selecting Search ➤ Find Next or Search ➤ Find Previous.

● **SHORTCUT**   Put the mouse pointer in the bottom half of the screen and press the left mouse button to scroll down through the file. Put the pointer in the top half of the screen to scroll up.

To View Graphic Files

1. Open a drive window and highlight the graphics image you want to view.

2. Select File ➤ View, or click on the View button in the button bar.

3. Use the keystrokes in Table 3.1 to manipulate the image. Press Esc when finished.

Table 3.1: Keystrokes for Manipulating Graphics

Keystroke	Action
H	Flip the image horizontally
V	Flip the image vertically
I	Invert the colors to their complements
+	Zoom in
−	Zoom out
]	Rotate 90 degrees clockwise
[	Rotate 90 degrees counterclockwise
Home	Return to original position and size

● **NOTE**   Remember that in the Viewer, though you can change how files appear on the screen, the actual file on the disk is not changed.

WINDOWS

The drive windows are at the heart of Norton Desktop for DOS. You can open up to eight on the desktop and use them to manage your files easily. If you have a mouse, drive window buttons appear on the left side of the desktop and include all available drives.

To Open a Drive Window

You can double-click on the drive icons buttons to open a drive window, or you can select Window ➤ Open Drive Window. Figure 3.4 illustrates the parts of a drive window.

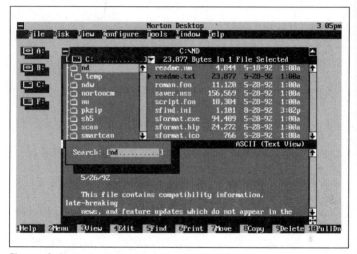

Figure 3.4: Parts of a Drive Window

PARTS OF A DRIVE WINDOW

The various parts of the drive window work together to make it easy to do most file operations with a click or two. The components of the drive window are listed below.

The **Status Bar** displays information about the drive or file(s) selected.

The **Drive Selector** is a combination box. It allows you to change drives without opening up another drive window. To change drives, highlight this box and key in the letter of the drive, or click on the drop-down box prompt button and select the drive.

The **Panes** make up the main body of the drive window. They display the selected drive's tree structure, a file list, and, optionally, with View Pane toggled on, the contents of the currently selected file. Select the panes you want open from the View menu.

The **Speed Search Box** is the quickest way to find a file or directory in either the Tree Pane or the File Pane. Note that you must start keying in characters for the Speed Search box to appear. When you begin keying in the name of the file or directory, the Speed Search box appears below the appropriate pane and the cursor bar moves to highlight the first file or directory that matches the keyed-in letters. If the Tree Pane is active, the Speed Search box works in the Tree Pane. If the File Pane is active, the Speed Search box works there. Press the Tab key to cycle the pane highlighter through the drive selector, Tree Pane, and File Pane.

If you have the DOS Background active, you will need to press Alt+F1 to display the Speed Search box.

To Move a Drive Window

If you are using a mouse, click on the title bar and, holding the mouse button down, drag the window to its new location. Release the button.

Using the keyboard, select Move from the Control menu. Use the arrow keys to move the window to the location you want. Press Enter when finished.

To Refresh the Drive Windows

You can set the drive windows to automatically update as moves, deletions, and so forth, are made. Select Configure ➤ Preferences ➤ Advanced, and check the box for Refresh Drive Windows Automatically.

If you do not have this option selected, you will need to select View ➤ Refresh when you want the drive window(s) to be completely updated.

To Resize a Drive Window

To adjust the size of a drive window, click on the resize button in the bottom-right corner of the window. (It looks like a four-headed arrow.) Holding the mouse button down, drag the corner of the window to the size you want. To enlarge a window to fill the screen, click on the maximize button in the top-right corner of the window, or choose Maximize from the Control menu.

To resize using the keyboard, select Size from the Control menu. Use the arrow keys to resize the window, and press Enter when finished.

To Configure the Panes

From the View menu, select from the following:

- **Tree Pane** to toggle the Tree Pane on and off.

- **File Pane** to toggle the File Pane on and off.

- **View Pane** to toggle the View Pane on and off.

- **Show Entire Drive** to replace the Tree and File Panes with a pane showing all the files on the drive and their locations.

To Filter the File Display in the File Pane

1. Select View ➤ Filter to bring up the Filter dialog box.

2. From the list in the File Type box, select the file types to display:

- Select **All Files** to show all the files. This is the Norton Desktop default setting.

- Select **Programs** to show all executable programs (.COM, .EXE, .BAT, .PIF, .BTM).

- Select **Documents** to show all document files (.DOC, .WRI, .TXT).

- Select **Custom** to define a custom filter.

3. If you chose Custom, fill in the combination box with the file specification(s) that you want displayed, or choose from a list of recent selections. (Note that Custom can be used with wildcards in the file specifications.)

4. If you do not want subdirectories to be shown, clear the Show Directories check box.

5. From the Attributes box, choose which files to display by attribute.

6. Select OK to confirm the choices, or Cancel to return to the previous configuration.

● **EXAMPLES**

- Toggle the **Hidden** attribute to blank to exclude hidden files.

- Toggle the **System** box to a check mark to display only System files.

- Choose **Custom**, then key in *.W?? to see all Lotus and Quattro Pro spreadsheet files.

- Choose **Custom**, then key in *.XLS *.W?? to see all spreadsheet files, including Excel files.

● **NOTE** To change a file's attributes, see "Attributes" above.

To Change the File Pane Detail

1. Select View ➤ File Details to bring up the File Details dialog box.

2. Select the file details that you want to see displayed in the File Pane. Items marked with a check will show in the pane. The sample line shows how the files will appear.

3. Select OK to confirm the choices, or Cancel to return to the previous configuration.

● **OPTIONS**

Icon Toggles the display of file icons. This option produces a visible result only when the display mode is All Graphical Controls under Configure ➤ Video/Mouse.

Size Toggles the inclusion of the file size in the display.

Date Toggles the inclusion of the file creation date in the display.

Time Toggles whether the file creation time is included in the display.

Attributes   Toggles whether the file display includes the file attributes (Hidden, System, Read Only, or Archive).

Directory   Toggles the display of the file's directory. (Active only when Show Entire Drive is on.)

To Change the Sort Order in the File Pane

1.   Select Sort By from the View menu.

2.   Use the mouse to highlight the file characteristic by which to sort, or select ascending or descending sort order. The display will be updated immediately.

● OPTIONS

Name   Sorts alphabetically by file name.

Extension   Sorts alphabetically by file extension.

Size   Sorts by file size.

Date & Time   Sorts by file creation date and time.

Unsorted   Displays files in DOS order.

Ascending   Displays files in alphabetical order, smallest to largest, or oldest to most recent.

Descending   Displays files in reverse alphabetical order, largest to smallest, or most recent to oldest.

● **NOTE**   By default, the primary sort order is by file name. If extension, size, or date is chosen as the primary sort, then the secondary sort is by name. The default sort is performed in ascending order (A before Z, 1991 before 1992, small before large) unless descending order is checked.

To Compare Windows

1.   Open a drive window for each of the two directories you want to compare. In each window, select the directory to be compared in the tree pane. The files of the directories should be displayed in the file panes of the respective windows.

2. Select Window ➤ Compare Windows. Read the message that appears, and select OK.

3. The two windows will be compared. All files that are different will be marked as "selected" in both panes.

Part Four

Tools and Utilities

CALCULATOR

The Norton Desktop for DOS provides a simple, four-function calculator that you can use for quick calculations.

To Use the Calculator

1. Choose Tools ➤ Calculator to pop up the calculator.

2. Use the mouse or the numeric keypad to enter numbers.

3. The functions can be entered either with the mouse or with the corresponding key. The keys and their functions are shown in Table 4.1.

4. To close the calculator, press Alt+F4 or select Close from the calculator's Control menu.

Table 4.1: Calculator Keys and Functions

Button	Keyboard	Function
+	+	Addition
−	−	Subtraction
*	*	Multiplication
/	/	Division
=	=	Computes the result
Clear	C	Clears the display and starts over
+/−	\ (also M, N, P, and S)	Changes the sign of the display
Backspace	Backspace	Clears the last digit in the display

CALENDAR

The Norton Desktop for DOS includes a simple, monthly calendar. This calendar allows you to attach a note to each day for reminders, to-do lists, and so on.

To Use the Calendar

1. Choose Tools ➤ Calendar to pop up the calendar.

2. By default, the current month and year will be shown, with the current day highlighted.

3. To add a note to the highlighted day, click on the Notepad button or press Alt+N. Key in the notes you want to attach to this day.

4. Select OK to attach the note to the highlighted day, or Cancel to abort the operation.

5. Days with notes attached will appear with a check mark.

● **NOTES**   To change the current day, click on the new one, or use the arrow keys. To change months, use the PgUp and PgDn keys, or Ctrl+← and Ctrl+→. To change years, use Ctrl+PgUp and Ctrl+PgDn. Home and End will take you to the first and last day of the month, respectively.

In the Notepad, press the Home key to go to the beginning of the current line. Press the Home key twice to go to the top of the screen. Press the End key to go to the end of the current line. Press the End key twice to go to the end of the screen entry.

LINK PCS

The Norton Desktop for DOS allows two PCs to be linked together for transferring files. This makes it easy to transfer files between any two PCs that have Norton Desktop installed, and you can even use a serial cable to install a limited version of Norton Desktop on one of the PCs if it doesn't yet have Norton Desktop installed.

The link between the two PCs may be over a network, as long as the network supports NetBIOS, or by way of a serial or parallel cable. One of the PCs must act as a server, while the other is the client; and while a PC is being used as a server, it cannot be used for anything else.

To Connect Two PCs

1. Decide on the physical connection to use, either a network or a cable, and if a cable, whether a serial or parallel cable.

2. Physically connect the two PCs. If you are using a network link, this means to log both machines onto the network. If you are using a cable link, connect the cable to the two PCs.

3. Start up Norton Desktop for DOS on both PCs. See "Desktop Link" in Part Two for information on cloning Norton Desktop for DOS onto the second computer.

4. Decide which PC will be the server and which the client. The server will provide files to the client, but the client will be the PC where you do all the work.

5. On the server PC, choose Disk ➤ Serve Remote Link. Select either Network Link or Desktop Link.

6. If you chose a network link, the Network Link dialog box will open. Choose which users on the network may log onto your system, and change the default file server if required. When you have finished, select OK to enable remote users to access your PC. The Connection Status dialog box will open, and your PC is now able to be accessed by those users on the network you have selected.

7. If you chose a cable (desktop) link, the Desktop Link message box appears.

8. From the client PC, start Norton Desktop and choose Window ➤ Open Window. Select either the Network Link or Desktop Link radio button, and then click on the Connect

button, or press Alt+E. If you are using a network link, the
Network Link Servers dialog box will open, showing a list
of available servers. Highlight the server to which you
want to connect, and select OK.

9. When the connection is established, the names of the
server's drives will appear in the Drive combination box.
Select the drive you want to access, and then select OK to
complete the connection.

10. A drive window will open with the selected drive shown.
From this window you can perform most file operations,
such as copy, delete, move, and so on, but you may not
launch an application.

11. When you are finished, close the window to end the
connection.

DISKETTE FUNCTIONS

Norton Desktop for DOS provides easy access to all your diskette
functions, including formatting, copying, labeling, and making a
diskette bootable. These diskette functions are substantially im-
proved over the plain DOS versions. They allow you, for example,
to make a diskette bootable even though DOS might not (because of
file-placement conflicts), and to copy even a high-density diskette
with only a single change of floppies.

To Copy a Diskette
Norton Desktop for DOS provides a diskette-copying utility that is
a substantial improvement over the DOS DISKCOPY program,
which can take several swaps of diskettes to completely copy a
high-density floppy. With Norton Desktop for DOS, the entire
source diskette is read in a single pass, and multiple copies of a diskette can be made without having to reread the diskette each time.

1. Select Disk ➤ Copy Diskette.

2. Click on the prompt buttons to select the source and destination drives. Click on OK.

3. You will be prompted to insert the source diskette. Click on OK after placing the diskette in the drive.

4. You will then be prompted to insert the target diskette. If the target diskette is not already formatted, you will be asked if you want to format it. Select Yes if you want to go ahead. Select No if you want to change the target diskette.

5. When you are finished copying, you will be asked if you want to make another copy of the source diskette. Select Yes if you do, No if you want to exit.

● **NOTE** A diskette can be copied only to a diskette of identical configuration. If you attempt to copy a diskette of one capacity to a diskette of a different capacity, you will get an error message. You can, however, make a file copy by opening the drive window for the source diskette, highlighting all the files, and dragging the files to the target diskette drive icon.

To Format a Disk or Diskette

The Norton Desktop for DOS provides a safe formatting utility that is far easier to use than DOS, and provides additional safeguards against accidentally formatting hard disks.

1. Select Disk ➤ Format Diskette.

2. Click on the prompt buttons at the side of the drop-down boxes to select one option from each of the following boxes:

Drive Select the drive to be formatted.

Size Select the size of the drive being formatted. If it is a hard disk, the size will be Fixed.

Format Type The *Safe* format uses its own formatting algorithm, which allows the recovery of data (using Un-Format) in the event of accidental formatting. The *Quick*

format is very fast because it merely rewrites the root
directory and File Allocation Table on the diskette and
thus cannot be used on a previously unformatted diskette.
A *DOS* format is the same DOS's format program and
erases the data completely and irrevocably. If you are
formatting new unformatted diskettes, you must use
the DOS format.

3. To set formatting options, click on the Configure button,
or press Alt+C. The Configuration window offers you the
following choices:

Floppy Drive   Lets you choose which floppy drive you
are configuring.

Type for Drive X: Where X is the drive you selected.
The choices are:

- Autodetect
- 5¼"
- 3½" 720K
- 5¼" 1.2MB
- 3½" 1.4MB
- 3½" 2.8MB

Prompt for Missing Diskettes   Modifies how Norton
Desktop checks to see if a disk is present in the drive.
Some laptops and other systems may require that this box
be left unchecked.

Allow Hard Disk Formatting   When checked, allows
Norton Desktop to format hard disks. Normally left unchecked for safety.

4. When you have made any choices desired, select
OK to enable them, or Cancel to return to the default
configuration.

5. Select any options that you want. Click on OK when you
have made your choices. Select Format or Exit.

● OPTIONS

Make Disk Bootable   Transfers DOS system files to the diskette so your computer can boot from them.

Save Image Info   Available only when using the Quick format. Safe format does the save automatically, and DOS leaves nothing on the disk. Norton Unformat can recover data from a diskette when unformat information has been saved.

Volume Label   May be keyed in here, if desired on the diskette.

Save Settings on Exit   When checked will save the current settings as the default.

To Label a Disk or Diskette

Labeling a floppy diskette can make it easier to identify, while labeling a hard disk provides an even more important security measure to prevent accidental formatting. The regular DOS format program will not format a labeled hard disk unless the exact label name is provided. Since Norton Desktop for DOS, unlike DOS, allows you to create labels that include lowercase letters, you can ensure that only someone with access to Norton Desktop for DOS can format your hard disk.

1. Select Disk ➤ Label Disk.

2. In the dialog box, click on the prompt button (or press Ctrl+↓) to see a list of the drives on your system and their assigned labels, if any.

3. Select the drive, and key in the label name in the Label text box. Select OK when finished.

To Delete a Disk Label

1. Choose Disk ➤ Label Disk.

2. Click on the prompt button and select the drive.

3.   Delete the current label in the Label text box. Select OK when finished.

To Make a Disk or Diskette Bootable

Norton Desktop for DOS allows you to make a disk bootable, even in situations where DOS's SYS command would fail.

1.   Choose Disk ➤ Make Disk Bootable.

2.   Select the drive to make bootable.

3.   Select OK to continue, or Cancel to abort the operation.

4.   If you selected a floppy drive, a window pops up asking you to put the diskette to be made bootable into the drive selected. Select OK after placing the diskette in the drive, or Cancel to abort.

5.   If you selected a hard drive, a confirmation window pops up, asking you to confirm your choice. Select Yes to make the drive bootable, or No to cancel the operation.

6.   When the operation is complete, an information window will pop up, telling you that the drive is now bootable. Select OK to acknowledge the message and return to the desktop.

NORTON MAIL

The Norton Desktop for DOS includes Norton Mail, a full-featured interface to MCI Mail. With Norton Mail, you can easily write MCI Mail messages and send them automatically to multiple MCI Mail accounts. You can automatically receive MCI Mail messages. You can use all the features of MCI Mail, including sending paper mail, Telex, electronic mail to MCI affiliates such as CompuServe, and faxes to any fax machine.

SETUP AND CONFIGURATION

Before you can begin to use Norton Mail, you need to have at least one MCI Mail account. Then you must configure Norton Mail so that it knows about your MCI Mail account(s) and your modem. Like the rest of the Norton Desktop for DOS, Norton Mail has a wide variety of configuration options to fine-tune how it works to your personal preferences.

● SETUP: OPTIONS

Where should newly created messages be placed?   Controls in which folder new (outgoing) messages are placed.

- **Out** places newly created messages in your Out Folder, from where they will automatically be sent the next time you log onto MCI Mail. This is the default.

- **Draft** places newly created messages in your Draft Folder, from where you must explicitly move them to the Out Folder before they will be sent.

- **Prompt User for Folder Name** will cause the Which Folder dialog box to pop up when you complete a new message, allowing you to decide where to put the new message.

Full Page Read   When checked causes messages you select to be displayed zoomed to full screen. With this option checked, you cannot unzoom.

Extended Message Info   When checked, the message description in each folder will include additional information about the message, such as when it was sent, the file size, and its file name.

Confirm Deletes   When checked, Norton Mail will require a confirmation whenever an Address Book entry or member of a mail list is deleted.

Include Message Text in Replies   When checked, the text of the original message will automatically be included in replies. When you are sending multiple messages to the same person on more than one subject, this can make the response easier to follow but makes the message longer.

Auto-Add Addresses   When checked, the sender's address from all mail received will be automatically added to your Address Book.

● SETUP: MCI TELEPHONE

MCI Phone Number lets you select either of two phone numbers:

- **Primary** by default; this number is 1-800-825-1515 and shouldn't be changed, since it is set up for automated programs such as Norton Mail.

- **Alternate** allows you to have an alternate phone number that can be used for special situations, such as when you are outside the U.S.

Phone Number Prefix lets you select a prefix to dial before dialing either the primary or alternate MCI phone number. The choices are:

- **None**
- **9,** dials a 9 and pauses two seconds before completing the dialing.
- **8,** dials an 8 and pauses two seconds before completing the dialing.
- **Custom** lets you insert a custom dialing prefix. A common choice might be ***70,** which would turn off call waiting in many parts of the U.S.

● SETUP: MODEM

Baud Rate   The choices are 300, 1200, 2400, and 9600 baud. The default is 1200 baud, which is correct for the default access phone number, 1-800-825-1515.

Dial Type   Select Tone or Pulse, depending on what your phone line supports.

Sound   Select On to hear the modem dialing, or Off to suppress any sounds from the modem.

COM Port   The choices are COM 1 through COM 4. Select the serial port to which your modem is attached.

Special Setup String Check this box to override the regular modem setup string and insert a special one. This is only for the advanced user, but may be necessary for calling from outside the U.S.

Modem Setup String The default should be fine for most users, but special cases or high-speed modems accessing the 2400-baud or slower port may require modifying the setup string. Consult your modem's documentation.

● SETUP: DIRECTORIES

The first time Norton Mail is run, default directories for the various mail folders are created. If you need to change this later, modify the entries here.

● SETUP: MCI ACCOUNTS

Norton Mail supports up to six MCI Mail accounts. Mail can be sent and received for all active accounts at the same time, but only a single account can be viewed at a time.

To Add New MCI Mail Accounts

1. If you haven't yet entered any accounts into Norton Mail, you will be prompted to create one when you initially start Norton Mail. If you have already entered Norton Mail, select Setup ➤ MCI Accounts.

2. Select New, and the Account Information dialog box will open.

3. Key the MCI Mail *login* name (not the full account name) into the MCI User Name text box. This will usually be the first letter of your first name, plus your full last name, without spaces.

4. Key the account's password into the MCI Password text box. This box will only show asterisks in place of the password.

5. Key the account's ID into the MCI ID text box. This is the number that looks like a telephone number.

6.   Check the Make Account Active check box if you want Norton Mail to start receiving and sending mail from this account.

7.   Select OK to set up the account, or Cancel to abort the operation.

To Edit an Existing MCI Mail Account

1.   Choose Setup ➤ MCI Accounts. Highlight the account you want to edit.

2.   Select Edit, and the Account Information dialog box will open.

3.   Modify the account information that you want to change. Check the Make Account Active–Send/Receive Mail box to include the account in your automatic send and receive group.

4.   Select OK to confirm the changes, or Cancel to abort the operation without keeping your changes.

To Delete an Existing MCI Mail Account

1.   Choose Setup ➤ MCI Accounts. Highlight the account you want to delete.

2.   Select Delete, and if you do not have Confirm Deletes on, the account is immediately deleted. If you do have Confirm Deletes on, you will be prompted to confirm the deletion.

3.   Select OK to exit the MCI Accounts dialog, which will make the deletions permanent, or press Esc to cancel the deletions.

To View an MCI Mail Account

1.   Choose Setup ➤ MCI Accounts. Highlight the account you want to view.

2.   Select View, and a message box pops up informing you that
     the account you have highlighted will now be viewed. Select
     OK or press Enter to view the account, or press Esc to return
     to the previous screen.

3.   Select OK to exit the MCI Accounts dialog. The account
     you have selected will be the account you are currently
     viewing.

● SETUP: PRINTER

The Setup ➤ Printer option calls up the main Configure Printer
dialog box. For details on configuring your printer, see "Printer" in
Part Two.

● SETUP: IMPORT

Norton Mail can import address books, account information, and configuration information from Norton Commander Mail (Version 3.0
only) and Lotus Express, Version 1.0. If you have previously used
either of these programs, you can simplify setting up Norton Mail by
importing information from your previous program.

To Import from Norton
Commander or Lotus Express

1.   Choose Setup ➤ Import.

2.   Select either Norton Commander or Lotus Express from
     which to import information.

3.   Key in the directories from which to import.

4.   Check which information you want to import. Configura-
     tion information will overwrite any existing configuration
     information, and account information will be added in
     order, up to the six accounts that Norton Mail supports.
     Address information from Norton Commander will be
     merged with the current Address Book, with the Norton
     Mail address information taking precedence.

5.   Select OK to confirm the import, or Cancel to return to the
     previous screen, without change.

MANAGING ADDRESSES

Norton Mail easily keeps track of your MCI Mail Address Book, and can even add addresses automatically, without any interaction on your part. Addresses can be an MCI Instant Address, a Telex address, a fax phone number, a paper mail address, or an electronic mail address for any of the other electronic mail systems that connect to MCI Mail.

To Automatically Add All Addresses

1. Choose Setup ➤ Options.

2. Check the Auto-Add Addresses check box.

3. Select OK to make the change active, or Cancel to abort the operation.

To Automatically Add Selected Addresses

1. Open the folder that contains the addresses you want to add.

2. Select the entries from which you want to add addresses. Either highlight the entry and press the space bar, or click on the entry with the right mouse button.

3. When all the addresses you want to add are selected, choose Addresses ➤ Auto-Add. The addresses will be automatically added to your address book.

To Manually Add an Address

1. Choose Addresses ➤ AddressBook or press Ctrl+A.

2. Select New to add a new address, or Copy to copy an existing address that is close to the one you want to add.

3. Select the method of message delivery from the Address Types dialog box. The choices are:

   • **Paper Mail** causes your message to be sent electronically to the nearest MCI Mail service center, and then be printed and delivered via the local postal service. Key in the full postal address in the boxes provided.

- **Telex** causes your message to be sent to any Telex machine. You can receive Telex messages at 650 plus your MCI ID. Key in the information required to send a Telex in the boxes provided.

- **EMS** causes your message to be sent to any other electronic mail system that is connected to MCI Mail, such as CompuServe. Fill in the necessary information in the text boxes provided.

- **FAX** causes your message to be sent electronically to any fax machine. Key in the name, the fax phone number, and the length of time to keep retrying (default is 4 hours).

- **MCI Instant** sends your message electronically to the other person's MCI Mail box. Key in the necessary information in the text boxes provided. It is best to include an MCI ID if possible, since this number is unique.

4. Key in the information required for the type of address chosen.

5. Select OK to add the address to your Address Book, or Cancel to return to the previous screen, with no changes made.

6. Select Close to confirm the changes you have made to your Address Book.

To Delete Addresses

1. Choose Addresses ➤ Address Book or press Ctrl+A.

2. Highlight the address you want to delete.

3. Select Delete to remove the address from your Address Book.

4. Select Close to confirm the changes you have made to your Address Book.

To Undelete Addresses (Current Session)

1. Choose Addresses ➤ Address Book or press Ctrl+A.

2. Highlight the address you want to undelete. In the column headed Type, it will show as Deleted.

3. Select Undelete and the address will be restored.

4. Select Close to confirm the changes you have made to your Address Book.

To Undelete Addresses (Previous Session)

1. Exit Norton Mail by choosing Folder ➤ Exit or pressing Alt+F4.

2. Bring up the DOS command prompt at the bottom of your Norton Desktop screen by pressing Ctrl+O if it isn't already present.

3. Key in **nmail /unerase** and press Enter.

4. Norton Mail will start. Follow the steps in the previous section, "To Undelete Addresses (Current Session)," to undelete the previously deleted addresses.

To Permanently Delete Addresses

1. Follow the steps above under "To Delete Addresses."

2. Exit Norton Mail, returning to the desktop.

3. Bring up the DOS command prompt at the bottom of your Norton Desktop screen by pressing Ctrl+O if it isn't already present.

4. Key in **nmail /purge** and press Enter. Norton Mail will start, and all your previously deleted mail addresses will be permanently and irrevocably erased.

RECEIVING MAIL

Norton Mail makes receiving your MCI Mail messages easy and automatic. You can even use the Scheduler to automatically remind you to read your MCI Mail at the same time every day.

To Collect Your MCI Mail Automatically

1. From the desktop, choose Tools ➤ Scheduler.

2. Select the date you want to begin automatically collecting your MCI Mail.

3. Select Add to bring up the Event Editor dialog box. Fill in the various text boxes to schedule this event. For more details, see the section on the Scheduler.

4. In the Command text box, key in the command **nmail /send**.

5. In the Event Type box, select Program.

6. Select OK to schedule the event, and then OK again to close the Scheduler window.

To Collect and Read Your MCI Mail Manually

1. Choose Mail ➤ Send/Receive, or press Ctrl+S.

2. Norton Mail will go online to MCI Mail, collect all the mail from all active MCI Mail accounts that you have set up, and send any mail in the Out Folder.

3. When the collection process is finished, you will be in the In Folder, with all new messages shown.

4. Highlight the first message you want to read, and select Read.

5. When you have finished reading the message, choose Mail ➤ Reply to reply to the message, or Close to return to the In Folder screen, where you can select additional messages to read.

6. Select Folder ➤ Exit when you are ready to leave Norton Mail.

SENDING MAIL

Norton Mail makes it easy to write letters, send faxes or Telexes, or write electronic mail messages to anywhere in the world from your desktop. You don't have to know the intricacies of how MCI Mail works, or all its commands. Just write your letter, select the address to which you wish it sent, and place the message in your Out Folder. Norton Mail handles the rest.

To Write a New Message

1.   Choose the New button at the side of any folder.

2.   The To text box will be highlighted. Begin typing in the recipient's name. The Address Book will open, with a search box. Keep typing in the name until the recipient's name is highlighted.

3.   Select OK to select the address as a recipient. For multiple recipients, select Add from the menu bar.

4.   For each address in step 3, select the type of message to send by choosing the Type button. The choices will depend on the information in your Address Book for that person.

5.   When you have selected all the recipients, choose OK.

6.   Select the cc field and repeat steps 3 to 5 to send "carbon copies" to additional people.

7.   Key in a subject, and then key in the body of the letter or message. You can make the editor full screen by pressing Alt+Z or selecting the Zoom button. Press Alt+Z again to unzoom the editor.

8.   Select OK to finish the message. Depending on how you have your options set, either you will be prompted for a folder in which to put the message, or the message will be placed automatically in your Out or Draft folder. If the message is not placed in your Out folder, you will need to move it to that folder to actually send it.

9.   Choose Folder and select the folder where the message was placed in step 8. Highlight the message you just wrote and choose Mail ➤ Move or press Ctrl+V to move the message to the Out Folder. (Skip this step if you have your options set so that new messages are automatically placed in your Out folder.)

10.   Choose Mail ➤ Send/Receive or press Ctrl+S to log onto MCI Mail and send the message.

NORTON MENU

Menus are easily created and updated using the Norton Menu. You can design a customized menu system for yourself or for an entire workgroup.

To Install Norton Menu as a Shell

1.   Use a text editor to open your AUTOEXEC.BAT file.

2.   Add NMENU as the last line of the file. The syntax is

Drive:\path\nmenu [/edit] [/run]

/Edit will allow you to edit and run menus. **/Run** will run menus but removes the menu bar so editing is not permitted. If the Password option is selected, the user will not be able to leave Norton Menu (see "To Customize Menus," below).

3.   Save your changes and reboot the computer to put them in effect.

To Start Norton Menu from within Norton Desktop for DOS

1.   Select Tools ➤ Menu (F2).

2.   The Main Menu will open. Select the Menu you want by clicking on it or highlighting it and pressing Enter.

3. To close a menu, use the Close command on the Control Box menu (Ctrl+F4).

To Start Norton Menu from the Command Line

At the command line, type **NMENU**. You can include the parameter **/edit** or **/run** (see "To Install Norton Menu as a Shell," above).

WORKING WITH MENUS

At the time of installation, you may have chosen to build Norton Menus for your computer. If you did not, you can at any time choose Tools ➤ Edit Menu ➤ File ➤ Autobuild. Norton Desktop for DOS will scan your hard disk(s) and assemble a menu for you automatically.

To Change a Menu Title

1. From within Norton Menu, select File ➤ Open.

2. The Open Menu dialog box opens. Select the Menu you want and click on OK.

3. Select Edit ➤ Menu Title. In the Edit Menu Title box, type in the new name for the menu. Select OK.

4. When you exit Norton Menu, you will be asked to confirm the changes you have made. Select Save to keep the changes, Discard to abandon the changes, or Cancel to return to Norton Menu.

● **NOTE** If you change the title of a submenu, you should also edit its entry in the main menu to match. Open the Main Menu, highlight the entry, and choose Edit ➤ Modify, or press Ctrl+E.

To Customize Menus

1. From within Norton Menu, select Options ➤ Preferences.

2. In the Preferences dialog box, check the options you want to adopt.

3.   When you are finished, select OK to save your choices or
Cancel to abandon them.

● OPTIONS

Confirm on Delete   Opens a dialog box asking the user to
confirm a requested deletion.

Autosave Files   Saves all changes to menus without asking
for confirmation. If this box is not checked, you will be asked if
you want to save changes you have made to a menu.

Ask for Edit/Run Password   Check this box, and the
dimmed-out Password button becomes available for use. Select
the Password button and type in a password. When this option
is checked, users without the password will not be able to edit
or exit the Norton Menu shell.

Check Program Names   This option should remain on unless you use NDOS or another program that assigns aliases to
your programs.

Menu Item Icons   Adds icon symbols next to menu items.

Autoassign Hotkeys   Check this box to have Norton Menu
automatically assign a hotkey to a menu item. You can then
press that key to select the item. Hotkeys are assigned in alphabetical order from A through Z and then in numerical
order from 1 through 9.

Security Alert Sound   A brief audible alarm will sound
when an invalid password is entered.

To Configure the Screen Saver and Clock

Directions for the Screen Saver and Clock under the Norton Menu
Options menu can be found in Part Two.

To Create a Menu

1.   From within Norton Menu, select File ➤ New.

2.   Type in the name for the new menu in the New Menu Title
text box.

3. Norton Menu will automatically assign a name to the new menu. The name will consist of the first eight letters of the menu title with the extension .NMF. If you want another name, click on the File button and type in the path and name you want.

4. Select OK when you are finished.

To Delete a Menu

1. From within Norton Menu, select File ➤ Delete.

2. The Delete Menu dialog box will open. To search through the list, start typing the name of the menu, and a speed search box will open.

3. Highlight the file you want to delete and select the Delete button. If you have checked the Confirm on Delete box in Preferences, you will be asked to confirm the deletion.

● **NOTE**   You will not be allowed to delete an open menu. Close the menu before you select File ➤ Delete.

To Distribute a Menu

Once you have built a menu on your computer, you can distribute it to other users. However, because all computers in your group will probably not be identically configured, you will need to take the following steps.

1. Create the menu. From within Norton Menu, select File ➤ Export. Select the menu from the Export Menu dialog box. Click on OK.

2. A file with the same name as the original menu but with the extension .NAB will be created in your Norton Desktop for DOS directory.

3. Copy the file to the Norton Desktop for DOS directory on the new computer.

4. On the new computer, select File ➤ Autobuild from inside Norton Menu.

5. The Autobuild or Update Norton Menus dialog box will open. Type in the name of the source file or click on Browse for a list of .NAB files. Click on OK to close the Browse box.

6. Type in the new menu's destination in the Path text box.

7. Select OK. The new menu will appear and be ready for use.

● **NOTE** When in .NAB format, the file can be edited manually using any text editor.

To Update Menus Automatically

If you have made changes in your directories or added new programs, you will need to update your menus.

1. From within Norton Menu, select File ➤ Autobuild.

2. In the Autobuild or Update Norton Menus dialog box, select Update an Existing Menu and click on OK.

The program will scan for new disk and path information and will update your menus accordingly.

WORKING WITH MENU ITEMS

Menus are the shells within which you can organize your work. Menu items fit within that shell and each item represents a part of your work environment.

There are three types of menu items. They are:

Program	A DOS program or DOS command that is executed from a menu
Submenu	A menu contained within another menu
Batch	A batch file that is run from a menu

To Add a Program Menu Item

1. Open a menu from within Norton Menu. Select Edit ➤ Add.

2.   The Add Menu Item dialog box opens, as shown in Figure 4.1. Click on Program in the Item Type box.

3.   In the Name text box, type in a descriptive name. Type in Help text on the next line. The Help text will appear at the bottom of the menu when this menu item is highlighted. Each line is limited to 32 characters.

4.   You can select a hotkey if Preferences is not set to automatically assign one. (See "To Customize Menus," above.)

5.   At the Command Line, type in the program's path, executable file name, and any other options needed. Or click on the Browse button, locate the file you want, and select it.

6.   Type in the Startup Directory, if needed. Some programs must launch from a particular directory to work properly. If you enter a particular directory here, Norton Menu will change to that directory before launching the program.

7.   Click on Password if you want the user to supply a password before running this item. Enter the password and confirm it. Select OK.

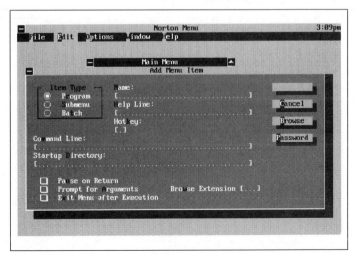

Figure 4.1: The Add Menu Item dialog box

8. Select the options at the bottom of the dialog box. Select OK to save your choices

● OPTIONS

Pause on Return Some applications display information on their final screen that you may want to see. Check this box and the program will pause at the final screen before returning to Norton Desktop.

Prompt for Arguments Check this box, and a dialog box for program arguments will open when the menu item is launched. You can enter information that the program needs before running.

Exit Menu after Execution After the menu item is run, Norton Menu terminates and you are returned to the desktop.

Browse Extension This option works when the Prompt for Arguments box is checked. Type in an extension here, and when the arguments dialog box opens, you can click on the Browse button to see a list of files with that extension.

To Add a Submenu

A submenu is a menu you call from another menu. The submenu must be created as a menu first. Then follow the steps below to make it into a submenu.

1. From within Norton Menu, open the menu to which you want to add a submenu. Highlight the appropriate menu item.

2. Select Edit ➤ Add. Select the Submenu radio button.

3. Type in a descriptive name in the Name text box. Enter a help line that will appear at the bottom of the menu box when this submenu is selected. Add a hotkey, if wanted.

4. Click on the File radio button and enter the file name if the one displayed automatically is not correct. Select OK when finished.

To Add a Batch Menu Item

A menu item can be created to run a batch file to launch applications and execute DOS commands.

1. From within Norton Menu, open the menu to which you
want to add the batch file menu item.

2. Select Edit ➤ Add. Select the Batch radio button under
Item Type.

3. Enter a descriptive name, Help line, and Hotkey.

4. Click on Password if you want to require a password to
run this item.

5. Type in the Batch File Text. Click on Zoom to get full-
screen Menu Editor.

● **NOTE** Batch files can contain up to 127 characters per line. If
your batch file is more than 100 lines, select File ➤ Save As. Enter a
file name with the extension .BAT. This will save memory. For
smaller batch files, Norton Menu can store the file internally.

6. If you are in the Menu Editor, select File ➤ Exit to NMenu.

7. Select OK when you are finished.

To Copy a Menu Item

To add a menu item that is very similar to an existing item, you can
use the copy command.

1. From within Norton Menu, select the menu item you want
to copy.

2. Select Edit ➤ Copy.

3. Open the menu where you want the copy to appear and
select Edit ➤ Paste. A copy of the item will appear. If you
are using the program to automatically assign hotkeys, the
hotkeys will change to reflect the new menu sequence.
You can now use Edit ➤ Modify to make any changes
you need.

To Delete a Menu Item

1. From within Norton Menu, highlight the menu item to delete.

2. Select Edit ➤ Clear.

3. The item is removed from the menu. If you are using the program to automatically assign hotkeys, the hotkeys will change to reflect the new menu sequence.

To Modify a Menu Item

1. From within Norton Menu, highlight the item you want to change. If the item is in a submenu, highlight the main menu first.

2. Select Edit ➤ Modify.

3. Type in the changes. Select OK when finished.

To Move a Menu Item

1. From within Norton Menu, highlight the menu item you want to move.

2. Select Edit ➤ Cut. You will be asked to confirm that you want to delete this item from this menu. Select OK.

3. Highlight the item that you want to be *under* the item you are moving. This can be in the same menu or another one.

4. Select Edit ➤ Paste, and the item will appear in the new location.

To Set a Password for a Menu Item

When you add or modify a menu item, the dialog box will include a password button. If a password is set for a menu item, the user will not be able to launch the item without providing the password.

1. In the Add or Edit Item dialog box, click on the Password button.

2. In the highlighted New Password box, type in the password you want. For additional privacy, the characters will appear as asterisks. Press Enter.

3. In the Confirm New Password box, type the password a second time. If the second entry does not match, you will be prompted to enter it again.

4. Press Enter or click on the OK button.

To remove a password, click on the Password button. Type in the old password and press Enter. In the New Password box, press Enter. You will be asked if you want to remove the password. Click on Yes. This item will no longer require a password to be launched.

NETWORK MESSAGE

Using Network Message, you can send a message to anyone on your network who is logged on to the same file servers as you are. Your message will be seen immediately unless:

- The recipient has cleared the Enable Network Messages check box in Configure ➤ Network and is in a DOS session or has launched an application from the desktop. However, as soon as the recipient returns to Norton Desktop, the message will appear.

- The recipient has used a network command to block network messages from appearing.

To Send a Network Message

1. Select Tools ➤ Network Message. The Network Message dialog box opens. Your name will automatically be shown on the From line.

2. Type your message in the Message text box. Your login name plus the message cannot be more than 58 characters.

3. Click on the Recipients button to open the Connected Network Users dialog box. The File Server combination box shows the file server name. Click on the prompt button to select another file server.

4. Select the names of recipients by clicking on them. Use the All button to select all connected users. Use the None button to deselect any currently selected names.

5. Select OK to leave the Connected Network Users box. Select OK in the Network Message dialog box to send the message.

● **NOTE**   If a recipient logged off the network before the message could be sent, a message will display informing you that the message was not delivered.

To Reply to a Network Message

1. In the Network Message dialog box, select the Reply button.

2. Your name will appear on the From line, and the name of the person who sent you the message will appear on the To line.

3. If you want to send your reply to additional people, select the Recipients button. Select the file server and names of recipients. Click on OK to exit the Connected Network Users dialog box.

4. Select OK in the Network Message box to send your reply.

NORTON ANTIVIRUS

The Norton AntiVirus program (NAV) is simple and easy to use. It provides excellent protection against all known viruses, as well as against those not yet discovered. Regular, free updates to the virus definitions are available from the Symantec BBS or in the Norton Utilities area of CompuServe (see "To Update Virus Definitions," below). NAV also has an intercept mode, which allows new viruses to be detected, even if they are not yet part of virus definitions in the main program, the AntiVirus Clinic.

NORTON ANTIVIRUS CLINIC

The Norton AntiVirus Clinic provides the primary interface for the user to check files, directories, and disks for viral infections, as well as to repair any damage.

To Scan a Drive or Drives

Norton AntiVirus will scan one or more drives, including net-worked drives, to search for the "signatures" of any of the viruses it knows. If you have enabled the option to check for unknown viruses, it will also check to see if any executable files have been modified since the last time you inoculated the drive.

1. If Norton AntiVirus is not open, open it by choosing Tools ➤ Norton AntiVirus.

2. Choose Scan ➤ Drive.

3. The Scan Drives dialog box will open.

4. Choose the drive or drives to scan for infections. Either choose individual drives using the Drives list box or click on the check boxes to select multiple drives. Here are your options:

- **All Floppy Drives** selects all floppy drives installed on this computer.

- **All Local Drives** selects all local drives, except for floppy drives.

- **All Network Drives** selects all network drives that are connected. (Access to this option may be turned on using Options ➤ Clinic.)

5. If this is the first scan of the current session, NAV will first scan the computer's memory for any resident viruses.

6. Once NAV has scanned all of the drives you have selected, it will open the Scan Results dialog box and report the number of files scanned and the number of viruses found.

If viruses were found, the option buttons for Repair, Delete, and Reinoc (Reinoculate) will now be available.

To Scan a Subdirectory or File

Norton AntiVirus will scan a file or directory to search for the "signatures" of any viruses it knows. If you have enabled the option to check for unknown viruses, it will also check to see if any executable files have been modified since the last time you inoculated them.

1.   Choose Scan ➤ File or Scan ➤ Directory to scan a file or a directory.

2.   Select the file or directory to scan. Click OK to scan the file or directory.

3.   If this is the first scan of the current session, NAV will first scan the computer's memory for any resident viruses.

4.   Once NAV has scanned the file or directory you selected, it will open the Scan Results dialog box and report the number of files scanned and the number of viruses found. If viruses were found, the option buttons for Repair, Delete, and Reinoc (Reinoculate) will now be available.

When a Virus Is Found

Norton AntiVirus will repair most infected files it finds, as well as repair the boot sector and partition table when they are infected. If NAV finds an infected file (or files) while scanning for a virus in the boot sector or partition table of the disk being scanned, it will report the files or areas infected. At this point, you can choose to repair the file or area, delete the file, or reinoculate it if NAV has reported a possible unknown virus. If the file is no longer required, click on the Delete button. NAV will ask you to confirm the deletion. Click Delete to delete just this file or Delete All to delete all similarly infected files. A final warning box will give you one last chance to cancel without deleting the file. Click Delete again to complete the deletion.

● **WARNING**   Files deleted by Norton AntiVirus are completely and irrevocably deleted. They can not be recovered by the undelete or unerase utilities.

If NAV has reported a virus in the boot sector of a floppy, in the partition table of a hard disk, or in a file that you still need and cannot easily replace, click Repair. NAV will open the Repair Files dialog box. Choose Repair to repair just the one file or Repair All to repair all infected files.

Finally, if the option is turned on to detect unknown viruses, NAV might report that a file may contain an unknown virus. If the file has been updated or otherwise changed since last inoculated, this will most likely be a false report; but if not, NAV may have just saved you from a disaster with a new virus strain. If you are absolutely certain that the file is safe and that it has been changed since the disk was last inoculated, click Reinoc to reinoculate the file. The Reinoculate Files dialog box will open. Click Reinoc to reinoculate only the single file or click Reinoc All to reinoculate all files reported as possibly being infected with an unknown virus. If you have any doubts about the file or have reason to suspect the file is infected, click Delete to delete the file. Unfortunately, Norton AntiVirus cannot repair a file infected with a virus it does not have in its definition list.

To Update Virus Definitions

Norton AntiVirus can only provide complete protection and repair capabilities against viruses for which it has definitions. Since new viruses are continually being introduced, it is important to keep Norton AntiVirus current. Symantec provides several methods for obtaining current definitions to update NAV. The choices are:

- The Symantec BBS, which provides current complete and update definition files. This can be accessed at 300 to 2400 baud or 9600 baud depending on your modem and communications software. The number for 300 to 2400 baud is (408) 973-9598 and for 9600 baud (408) 973-9834.

- CompuServe. The NAV-IBM Library section of the Norton Utilities Forum also provides current complete and update definition files. Log onto CompuServe using your normal procedures and at any ! prompt type **GO NORUTL** to reach the Norton Utilities Forum.

- Faxline. You can get a fax of the new virus definitions by calling (310) 575-5018 from a touch-tone phone. Instructions and assistance for the Faxline are available by calling (310) 477-2707.

- Virus Definition Update Disk Service, which provides updated definitions for a nominal fee (currently $12.00 plus shipping, handling, and taxes). You can order disks by calling (800) 343-4714 extension 756.

Once you have the new definition file, you can update your copy of Norton AntiVirus.

1. Open the Norton AntiVirus Clinic by choosing Tools ➤ Norton AntiVirus.

2. Choose Definitions ➤ Modify List or Definitions ➤ Load from File, depending on whether you have a hard copy of the new definitions or a .DEF file.

3. If you are modifying the list based on hard copy of the new definitions, the Modify List dialog box will open. Select Add to open the Add Virus Definition dialog box and type in the new definition. Click OK when you have finished entering the definition, and then click OK to accept the changes. Depending on which version of the AntiVirus Intercept you are using, the new definitions may not take effect until you reboot.

4. If you are updating Norton AntiVirus by loading the definitions from a file, the Load from File dialog box will open. Use the browse boxes to locate and select the new definition file and then click OK to load the new definitions into Norton AntiVirus. Depending on the version of the AntiVirus Intercept you are using, the new definitions may not take effect until you reboot.

To Inoculate against Unknown Viruses

Norton AntiVirus can detect changes in an executable file, which may indicate that it has become infected by a virus. This is even true for viruses it doesn't have definitions for. In order for NAV to detect such file changes, you must inoculate the disk.

1. Choose Options ➤ Global and check the Detect Unknown Viruses and Auto Inoculate boxes.

2. Scan the drive you want to inoculate, and Norton will automatically inoculate the files on that drive while it is scanning them for currently defined viruses.

To Uninoculate a Drive

If you update the programs on a drive, the inoculation data for that drive becomes outdated and will give false reports of possible virus infection. To correct this, you need to uninoculate the drive and then reinoculate it. It is best to do this when you have recently up-dated your virus definitions so that you are unlikely to accidentally inoculate a file that is already infected by an unknown virus.

1. Choose Tools ➤ Uninoculate.

2. Select the drive(s) to uninoculate.

3. Click OK to begin the uninoculation.

4. If NAV was successful in uninoculating the drive(s), the Uninoculate Results information box will open. If it was unable to uninoculate the drive, usually because the drive was not inoculated, a warning box will inform you of the failure.

● OPTIONS: CLINIC

Allow Repair   Permits the user to select repair of infected files when Scan detects a virus.

Allow Delete   Permits the user to select deletion of infected files when Scan detects a virus.

Allow Reinoc   Permits the user to select reinoculation of files that have been reported as having a possible unknown virus. *Use this option with caution!*

Allow Cancel   Permits the user to cancel out of the Scan Results dialog box, even if a virus has been detected.

Allow Repair All   Permits the user to select a wholesale repair of multiple infected files.

Allow Delete All   Permits the user to delete all infected files when multiple files are affected.

Allow Reinoc All   Permits the user to simultaneously reinoculate all files that have been reported as having a possible unknown virus. *Use this option with extreme caution!*

Allow Scanning of Network Drives   Permits the user to scan all drives on a network, not just local ones.

● **OPTIONS: INTERCEPT**

Enable Beep Alert   Sounds a distinctive beep when a virus is encountered.

Enable Popup Alert   Displays an information box that describes the virus detected and optionally permits the user to use the file. The length of time this popup box stays on screen can be entered in the Seconds to Display Alert Box text box. An entry of 0 seconds will leave the box displayed until it is acknowledged.

Enable Log to File   Logs all virus reports to a file. Enter the file name for this log in the text box.

Allow Proceed   Allows the user to load an infected program after acknowledging the popup box.

Allow Reinoculate   Allows the user to reinoculate a file which is reported to have an unknown virus. *Use this option with caution!*

● **OPTIONS: GLOBAL**

Detect Unknown Viruses   Uses inoculation data to determine if an executable file has changed.

Auto Inoculate   Automatically stores inoculation data for each file the first time it is accessed. Scanning a file will cause it to be inoculated.

Scan Executables Only   Scans executable files only. Data files are ignored.

Network Inoculation Directory   Tells Norton AntiVirus where on the local drives to store the inoculation data for networked drives.

Virus Alert Custom Message   Allows you to have your own message in the popup box when Norton AntiVirus detects a virus.

● OPTIONS: SET PASSWORD

This allows you to set a password on all the other options to prevent unauthorized users from modifying the program options.

NORTON VIRUS INTERCEPTS

Norton AntiVirus comes with three memory-resident antivirus programs, which enable it to detect a virus before it infects other files. The programs are NAV_.SYS, NAV&.SYS /B, and NAV&.SYS. In order to provide protection against an infection spreading from its source, one of these should be loaded as a device driver in your CONFIG.SYS file.

```
DEVICE=C:\ND\NAV_.SYS
DEVICE=C:\ND\NAV&.SYS /B
DEVICE=C:\ND\NAV&.SYS
```

Whichever of these device drivers you choose, it should be loaded as early in your CONFIG.SYS file as possible to provide maximum protection. If you use QEMM or another memory manager that permits programs to be loaded into high memory, however, the device driver line must come *after* the line that loads the memory manager.

The first option, NAV_.SYS, uses approximately 38K of memory but provides the most comprehensive protection. Each application is scanned when it is launched, and files are scanned when they are copied. It also provides protection against boot sector and partition table viruses.

The second option, NAV&.SYS /B, uses approximately 4K of memory and provides the best compromise between protection and size. It scans applications when they are launched and can detect boot sector viruses on floppy drives.

The third option, NAV&.SYS, uses only 1K of memory but will scan only when an application is launched. It will not detect boot sector viruses on infected floppies.

● **WARNING**   You must temporarily remove the Norton Virus intercept from your CONFIG.SYS file and reboot before creating a STACKER drive, or data loss may occur.

NORTON BACKUP

Norton Desktop for DOS includes Norton Backup for DOS, a full-featured, flexible backup program that can be configured easily for novice and advanced users alike. Norton Backup for DOS is fully compatible with Norton Backup for Windows, and both programs can read and restore files from each other. Further, Norton Backup supports several commonly used tape drives, including QIC-40 and QIC-80 types.

USING NORTON BACKUP THE FIRST TIME

Before Norton Backup can run on your computer, it needs to know what kind of floppy and tape drives you have, and how your computer responds to certain commands. To get this information, the first time you start Norton Backup it will automatically run a series of tests to determine how your hardware operates, and it will check to make sure that its options are correctly set to ensure reliable backups. It is strongly recommended that you complete *all* of these tests before attempting to make backups.

To Back Up the First Time

1.   Select Tools ➤ Norton Backup.

2.   An alert box will pop up, advising you that the Norton Backup has not been configured yet. Select Start Configuration to proceed.

3. The Program Level dialog box will open. Choose the desired program level. See "Options: Program Level" below for details about the different choices. Select OK to continue.

4. The Video and Mouse Configuration dialog box will open. Make any changes desired here and then select OK to proceed.

5. Backup will next try to determine what kind of floppy-disk drives you have on your computer. First, it will pop up an information box telling you to remove any floppy disks from their drives. Do so and select Start Test in this box. A message box will open showing the configuration Backup has found. Select OK to proceed.

6. If you have a tape drive, an information box opens asking you to remove any tapes so the driver can be configured and Norton Backup can determine if it can talk successfully to the drive. Remove the tape and select Start Test. The Backup Devices dialog box will now show the tape-drive type found. Select OK to proceed.

7. Next, Norton Backup will run several tests, including a speed test, a DMA test, and a small compatibility test to the floppy drive (and another to the tape drive, if you have one).
Press Enter as required to step through the tests.

8. When Norton Backup gets to the floppy-disk compatibility test, it does a two-disk "backup and compare" cycle. It first does a backup of a set of its own files and then compares the backed-up files against the originals. Select Start test to begin.

9. An Alert box will open, advising you that the compatibility test will pause to allow you to select which drive and disk density to use to perform the test. Press Enter or click on Continue to continue the test.

10. Select the drive letter and density to use for the test, and press Enter or click on OK to continue.

11. Follow the prompts to run the backup and compare. Note that if you change disks within 15 seconds of the initial

prompt, Backup will detect the change automatically.
When you have completed the test, Norton Backup will
inform you if the test was successful.

12. If you have a tape drive, Backup will next perform a
similar small backup and compare to the tape drive.
Again, select Start Test to begin.

13. When all the tests have been successfully completed, Norton Backup will prompt you to make several changes in
your CONFIG.SYS and AUTOEXEC.BAT files. Save these
changes, and Norton Backup will then scan the current
hard drive to create a default backup set.

14. Finally, when the tests have concluded successfully, you
can adjust any of the configuration options listed below,
by selecting the Configure button from the main window.

CONFIGURATION

To open the Configure window, click on the Configure button. This
will allow you to make changes to the program level, floppy- and tape-
drive type, disk-logging method, catalog-file path, and DMA speed.
Any changes made here will apply to all operations in Backup.

Also, if you change any of your hardware after the initial installation and running of Norton Backup, you should rerun the following configuration tests by clicking on the appropriate buttons.

● OPTIONS: PROGRAM LEVEL

Preset   Governs all options within the Backup, Compare,
and Restore windows, except the drive to which to back up or
from which to restore/compare.

Basic   Allows limited access to changing options within the
Backup, Compare, and Restore windows.

Advanced   Allows full access to all options within the Backup, Compare, and Restore windows.

● OPTIONS: VIDEO AND MOUSE

Screen Colors   Allows you to change to any of several different predefined palettes, or to custom choose your colors.

Display Lines   Allows you to choose from several different lines per screen, with the choices dependent on the video card installed.

Graphical Display   Allows you to choose to have a graphical mouse, graphical dialogs, and so forth.

Mouse Options   Allows you to set the double-click speed, sensitivity, acceleration, and so forth, of the mouse.

● OPTIONS: BACKUP DEVICES

Auto Config   Allows you to reconfigure your drive(s) automatically.

Floppy Drive A   Allows you to manually reconfigure the floppy drive. If you have two drives, there will be a choice for the B drive as well. Options for each floppy-disk drive are:

> **Not Installed**
> **360 Kb 5¼"**
> **720 Kb 5¼"**
> **720 Kb 3½"**
> **1.2 Mb 5¼"**
> **1.44 Mb 3½"**

Tape drive   Allows you to manually configure the tape drive. Choices are:

> **Not Installed**
> **40 Mb ¼" cartridge**
> **80 Mb ¼" cartridge**

● OPTIONS: CONFIGURATION TESTS

Disk Log Strategy

- **Fastest** works with most disk drives, but may not work with networked or substituted drives.

- **Most compatible** works with all DOS devices and requires less memory than Fastest option.

- **High Speed** works with most 386 and above computers but may not work with some older or less than 100 percent compatibles.

- **Low Speed** works with all computers, but is substantially slower than the high-speed option.

High Speed CPU Warning   When checked, Norton Backup will issue a warning when you start a backup, compare, or restore without first changing your computer to its slower speed. Useful for some older clones that can not access the floppy drives except at the slower speed.

Compatibility Test   Runs a backup and compare test cycle to ensure dependable backups to the tape or floppy-disk drive of your choice.

DMA Test   Performs a test of DMA operation to determine the correct setting for the Direct Memory Access options.

THE BACKUP WINDOW

Norton Backup allows you a wide range of ways to handle backups. You can preconfigure your backups and run them automatically by adding parameters to the command line, then add them to the Pull-down Menus, or to Norton Menu to be invoked manually at the end of the day, or have Scheduler automatically run your backups for you.

You can create a variety of predefined setup files that back up different groups of files, or you can interactively select the files to back up and then store them in a new setup file if you wish.

In addition, you can control the number and type of possible options for each backup, from virtually none (except for choosing a predefined set of files), with the program level set to Preset, to a full range of options for compression technique, format type, and so forth, with the program level set to Advanced. Finally, if you put Norton Backup on your button bar, you can back up files by highlighting them in a drive window and dragging them to the Backup button on the button bar.

Types of Backups

There are three basic types of backups. They are:

- Full
- Incremental
- Differential

In addition, there are copy versions of the Full and Incremental backup types that do not change the archive bit of the files that are backed up, nor do they affect the backup cycle settings. These two options are useful primarily as means of transferring files between computers and will not be discussed again.

A Full backup is one made of all the files that you select. This can be all the files on the hard disk (a total backup), all the files in a particular drive or directory, or some other reasonable subset of the files on your hard disk. A Full backup turns off the archive bit on the backed-up files and begins a backup cycle. You can save the set of files selected for backup as a setup file, and reuse them later.

An Incremental backup includes all the files in the selected set that have changed since your last Full or Incremental backup. An Incremental backup turns off the archive bit of each file that has been backed up. In the event of disaster to your hard disk, you must restore the Full backup set and *all* Incremental backup sets. Do not reuse incremental diskettes between Full backups, because a complete restore requires the full set plus *all* the incrementals.

A Differential backup includes all the files in a selected set that have changed since the last Full backup. A Differential backup does not turn off the archive bit. In order to restore files to your hard disk, you need restore only the last Full backup plus the most recent Differential backup. You can reuse all Differential backup diskettes except the most recent, unless you want to maintain multiple versions of the changed files.

Program Level

There are three program levels for Backup: Preset, Basic, and Advanced. The program level selected controls the number and type of options that are available to the user in the Backup window. The program level is set in the Configure window.

● OPTIONS: PRESET

The only options available in the Norton Preset Backup window are the setup file to use, which is selected using the Preset Backups list box, and the floppy-disk or tape drive to use, which is selected using the dialog box that appears when you click on the Backup To button.

● OPTIONS: BASIC

The Basic program level gives the user access to all the options at the Preset level plus the ability to create or change setup files (see "Setup Files" below); create and run macros (see "Macros" in the *Automating Backups* section); change file selections (see "Selecting Files" below); change the Backup type (see "Types of Backups," above). You can access the following toggles via the Options button, which are set separately for tape and disk backups:

Verify Backup Data   Compares the source file and the backed-up file. This slows the backup process but greatly improves the confidence level.

Compress Backup Data   Compresses the files as they are backed up, saving disk space and reducing the time needed for backup.

Password Protect Backup Sets   Prevents you from restoring backed-up files without a password, even when Backup is run automatically from the Scheduler.

Perform an Unattended Backup   Performs automatic tape backups without user intervention. Prompt boxes are still displayed for 15 seconds, but if the user doesn't respond, an automatic response is used to continue the backup.

Retry Busy Network Files   Instructs Backup to wait for busy files before continuing the backup. This can cause substantial slowdowns on networks if backups are scheduled at busy times.

Generate a Backup Report   Generates a report on the files, options, and times of the backup, which is stored on the disk in

the setup-file directory with the same name as the setup file
and the extension .RPT.

Audible Prompts (Beep)   Beeps whenever an action is required on your part or an error condition occurs.

Protect Active Backup Sets   Will warn you if you attempt to
back up to a floppy disk or tape that contains part of an active
backup set from your computer. It will *not* warn you if the disk
is from another computer.

Keep Old Backup Catalogs   Keeps old backup catalog files
on the hard disk. This can be useful if you use backups to keep
track of version information and you want to restore an older
version of a file without having to rebuild the catalog from the
disks.

Quit After Backup   Automatically quits when the backup is
completed.

At the Basic program level, there are additional options available
when you click on the Backup To button. The choices available will
depend on the destination selected but may include:

Prompt Before Overwriting Used Diskettes   Displays an
alert box if you insert a diskette that has been used before. This
allows you to replace the diskette with a new one or to verify
that it is alright to overwrite the current one. (Not an option for
tape backups.)

Use Error Correction on Diskettes   Writes additional error-
correction information on the diskettes to provide an extra
level of data integrity. Note, however, that this error correction
information will use from 11 to 13 percent of the available disk
space.

Proprietary Diskette Format   Uses a special format that will
make it possible to store more information on each diskette
and that will make the backup faster after the first time. The
first time a diskette is used with this option *on*, the backup will
be slower, since the diskette must be reformatted.

Always Format Diskettes   Will always format diskettes,
even if they are already formatted. This will slow down backups substantially, but does provide an extra measure of
reliability.

Backup to a Single DOS Component File   Creates a single file. This would be the normal option when backing up to a DOS drive or path. However, if the backup will later be transferred to floppy disks, leave this option off, and Norton Backup will create multiple backup files, each one no larger than the maximum-size floppy available on your system.

Display Directory Listing Prior to Backup   Displays a listing of the contents of the floppy disk (when selected as a backup to "DOS Drive and Path") or tape. This allows you to replace the floppy or tape with another if you accidentally selected one that you want to preserve.

Append Backup Data to Tape   Appends the current backup after any other backups on the tape. When off, Backup overwrites any other information on the tape.

Store Copy of Catalog on Tape   Stores a copy of the catalog file on the tape. This catalog is stored in a separate volume on the tape, which can cause the backup to take longer.

Always Format Tapes   Reformats the tape prior to backing up. This takes an additional 40 minutes with QIC-40 format tapes, but increases the reliability of the backup.

● OPTIONS: ADVANCED

With the program level set to Advanced, all the options that are available at the Basic level remain available, with the following additions or changes when the Options button is selected:

Data Verification   Offers three choices for data verification:

- **Off** which does no checking.
- **Sample Only** which checks every eighth track.
- **Read and Compare** which checks every byte.

Data Compression   Offers four choices for the level of compression:

- **Off** which does no compression.
- **Save Time** which does compression only while the Central Processing Unit (CPU) is idle, waiting for the floppy drive.

- **Save Space (Low)** which tends to result in greater compression than Save Time but runs slower on slow computers.

- **Save Space (High)** which minimizes the amount of disk space used but generally runs slower than the other options, except on the fastest computers.

Unattended Backup   Offers five different time frames:

- **Off** which will wait for user input at all prompts.

- **On, No Delay** which doesn't pause at all for user input.

- **On, 5 Second Delay** which pauses for 5 seconds at user prompts before continuing.

- **On, 15 Second Delay** which pauses for 15 seconds at user prompts before continuing (the default).

- **On, 60 Second Delay** which waits a full minute for input before continuing.

Audible Prompts   Offers four choices:

- **Off** which provides no audible prompting when user action is required.

- **Low** which emits a low, buzzer sound when user action is required.

- **High** which emits a higher, beep sound when user action is required.

- **Chime** which emits a four-tone clock chime when user action is required.

Network   Offers additional busy file options in Advanced Mode for users of Netware 286/386. You can choose to send a message to the user of a busy file (Netware 286 only) or select from four options for retrying busy files. These are:

- **For [1:00..] Hours** lets you choose how long to keep trying to back up busy files. The default is 1 hour.

- **Until [12:00..]** lets you specify a time of day to stop trying to back up busy files.

- **Until No Longer Busy** will keep trying indefinitely. This is the same as the Retry Busy Network Files option in the Basic Mode.

- **Do Not Retry** will skip any busy files and not attempt to back them up.

Reporting   Offers several options when running in Advanced mode. When any of the Include in Report options are on, an ASCII report is saved in the directory specified for catalog files. The report will have the same name as the .SET file but will have an .RPT extension. Thc choices are:

- **Backup Options Settings** includes the backup settings that were used for the backup.

- **List of Processed Files** includes the full file name and path of each file backed up.

- **All Error Messages** includes all the error messages for any files that were skipped.

- **Summary of Backup Statistics** includes the estimated and actual time, files, and bytes backed up.

- **Append each new backup report to the previous report** appends new reports after an existing one instead of overwriting it.

At the Advanced program level, there are options available in addition to ones available at the Basic level when you click on the Backup To button. The choices available will depend on the destination selected but may include:

Overwrite Warning   Several additional overwrite options are available, depending on the backup media selected. They are:

- **Off** which gives no warning before overwriting previously used diskettes.

- **Regular DOS Diskettes** which warns you before overwriting any DOS diskette that contains data.

- **Norton Backup Diskettes** which warns you before overwriting any diskette that contains Norton Backup data.

- **Any Used Diskette** which warns you before overwriting any diskette that contains any data at all.

- **Always Append** which places the current backup after whatever is already on the tape.

- **Always Overwrite** which overwrites anything currently on the tape and begins from the front of the tape.

- **Overwrite on Full Backup Only** which will append Differential or Incremental backups but will overwrite on a Full backup.

Error Correction Offers three different levels of error correction when backing up to floppy disks. The choices are:

- **Off** which records no error correction information on the floppy, maximizing the space available for data.

- **Standard** saves sufficient information to recover from any two adjacent sectors that are damaged.

- **Enhanced** saves enough information to recover from a hole punched through the diskette right on a sector boundary. This option is only valid when using regular DOS-formatted floppy disks. When the Proprietary Diskette Format option is selected, this will only give the same level of error correction information as the Standard option.

Backup File Size is available only when you are backing up to a DOS path. It allows you to choose the size of the backup file, which can make later transfers to diskette much easier. The options are as follows:

- **Use Best DOS fit** which uses the maximum size available

- **360 K Component Size**

- **720 K Component Size**

- **1.2 Mb Component Size**

- **1.44 Mb Component Size**

SETUP FILES

Setup files are files that you create to define a group or set of files to back up. For example, you could have a setup file that effects a total backup of your hard disk. This set would include all drives and directories on your hard disk. Another set might hold all your word-processing files, including all the files in your C:\WP51\FILES subdirectory. Still another might be the files required for your monthly newsletter, which could include spreadsheet, word-processing, database, and Pagemaker files. Each of these might have a different backup strategy associated with it. You might do total backups only once a month with weekly incrementals, for example, but do weekly Full backups of your word-processing files, with Differential backups on a daily basis. Your newsletter, on the other hand, might get a Full backup once a month after you finish it, with nothing in between.

To Open a Setup File

1.   Click on Backup, Compare, or Restore.

2.   Select File ➤ Open Setup. The Open Setup File dialog box will open.

3.   Choose from the list of available setup files and select Open to open the file.

To Create a New Setup File

1.   Click on the Backup button.

2.   Click on the Select Files button.

3.   Select the files that you want to include in this backup set. For details on selecting files, see "To Select Files To Backup," below.

4.   When you have completed your file selection, select OK to return to the Backup window.

5.   Select the type of backup you want from the Backup Type box.

6.   Select the destination for the backup (Backup To). Set the destination-related options you want saved as part of the setup.

7.   Click on the Options button.

8.   Select the options you want saved as part of this backup set.

9.   Select File ➤ Save Setup As.

10. Key in the new file name for this setup file. Be sure to include the .SET extension.

11. Select Save to save the new setup file, or Cancel to abort the save.

To Change an Existing Setup File

1. Click on the Backup button.

2. Open the setup file you want to modify, or choose Setup File and select the file you want to modify in the dialog box.

3. Make the changes you want to make to the file selection, backup type, backup device, and so forth.

4. Select File ➤ Save Setup to save the changes, or select File ➤ Save Setup As to create a new setup file.

To Select Files to Backup

1. Click on the Backup button to open the Backup window.

2. Click on the Select Files button to open the Select Backup Files window. This window, shown in Figure 4.2, has two panes—a Tree Pane and a File Pane—as well as a button bar at the bottom.

3. Select directories for backup by using one of the following methods:

   • Double-click or right-click on the name of the directory in the Tree Pane to toggle the selection of its files on or off.

   • Highlight the directory in the Tree Pane and then press the spacebar to toggle the selection of its files on or off.

   • Highlight the directory in the Tree Pane and then press Ins to select the files in that directory or Del to deselect the files in that directory. *Use this method if recording a macro for later playback, since its behavior is independent of the current state.*

4. You can select individual files in the File Pane using the same methods used in step 3 for directories.

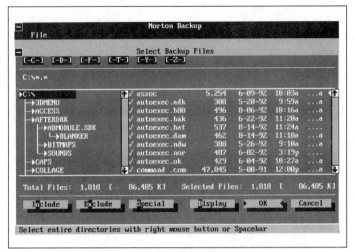

Figure 4.2: The Advanced Select Backup Files window

5. If you are running at the Advanced program level, you can select groups of files meeting specific criteria using the Include, Exclude, and Special buttons in the button bar at the bottom of the window.

6. Save your selections by clicking on the OK button or abandon them by clicking on the Cancel button.

● OPTIONS: BUTTON BAR

Include Available only at the Advanced program level, opens up the Include Files dialog box, shown in Figure 4.3. Fill in the path for files to include in the Path text box and the file specification in the File text box. Check the Include All Subdirectories box to include all subdirectories in the selection. Then click on OK to add this group of files to those selected for backup. Click on the Edit Include/Exclude List to open a dialog box that will let you see and edit the list of file groups included or excluded. (You will lose your entries in the Path and File text boxes when you choose this option.) Within the Edit

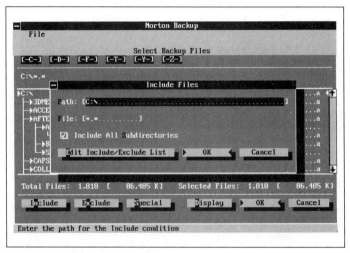

Figure 4.3: The Include Files window

Include/Exclude List dialog box, you can:

- **Edit** an existing file group selection by highlighting it and clicking on the Edit button. This lets you include or exclude the files described, apply the selection to sub-directories of the path, change the drive and path, and apply a file specification filter.

- **Delete** a group of files from the Include/Exclude list by highlighting its description and clicking on the Del=Delete button or pressing the Del key.

- **Copy** an Include/Exclude filter by highlighting it and pressing the Ins key or clicking the Ins=Copy button.

Exclude   Available only at the Advanced program level, behaves in the same way as Include, except that one is removing files from the backup selection, not adding them.

Special   Available only at the Advanced program level, opens the Special Selections dialog box shown in Figure 4.4. This box allows you to limit your backup to files that fall within a range of dates and to exclude special files such as copy-protected, hidden, system, and read-only files. When you use this option, you must

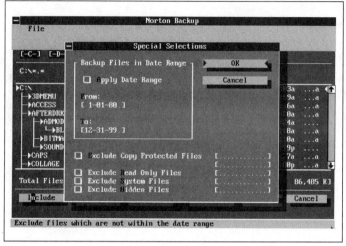

Figure 4.4: The Special Selections window

still select the files using one of the other methods, but any files that
are excluded here will not be selected.

Display   Opens the Display Options dialog box. With this box,
you can choose the order in which files are displayed, whether to
group selected files together, and whether to show only certain files
in the display.

● OPTIONS: MENU

File, View opens a View window to let you view the contents
of the highlighted file.

File, Delete allows you to delete the highlighted file.

File, Copy allows you to copy the selected files in the File pane
to a floppy disk as a regular DOS file.

THE COMPARE WINDOW

The Compare window allows you to compare previously backed-
up files against the files on your hard disk. Use this to verify the integrity of a backup without actually restoring the files. To reduce the

time it takes to do a comparison, you can select the files to compare
so that you check only irreplaceable files.

To Compare Files

1. Click on the Configure button to open the Configure
    window.

2. Select the program level to use. Choose OK, to make the
    change for the current session, or Save to save the pro-
    gram level permanently.

3. Click on the Compare button to switch to the Compare
    window. (At the Preset program level, click on the Restore
    button to bring up the Restore window. You will choose
    Start Compare to start the comparison.)

4. Select the backup catalog to use.

5. Select the drive to compare.

6. Select the files to compare by clicking on the Select Files
    button and selecting the files in the Select Compare Files
    window.

7. Repeat steps 5 and 6 if the comparison involves multiple
    drives.

8. Select from where the files are being compared.

9. If using the Basic or Advanced program level, select the
    location of the files to which you want to compare.

10. If using the Basic or Advanced program level, click on the
    Options button to set any options.

11. If you're using the Basic or Advanced program level and
    you want to use a catalog not on the default drive and
    directory, or you need to rebuild or retrieve a catalog,
    select the Catalog button.

12. Click on the Start Compare button to begin the com-
    parison process.

Program Levels

The same three program levels are available as in the Backup window—Preset, Basic, and Advanced—and they are set in the Configure window. Each higher step provides increased control over the details of the way Backup works. At the Preset level, the Compare and Restore windows are combined into a single Restore window.

● OPTIONS: PRESET

Backup Set Catalog   Contains the names and descriptions of the master catalogs created when backup sets were made. Choose the backup set you want to compare.

Select Files   Opens the Select Compare Files window, where you can select the files to compare.

Compare From   Allows you to choose the device to use for the compare operation.

● OPTIONS: BASIC

The Basic and Advanced comparison options are very similar. At the Basic program level, the options include all the options at the Preset level plus the following:

Backup Set Catalog   Lets you choose from individual catalogs or from the master catalog from each backup set.

Compare To   Lets you select the location with which to compare the backup set. The choices are:

- **Original Locations**
- **Other Drives**
- **Other Directories**
- **Single Directory**

Options   Lets you choose to toggle five additional options:

- **Perform an Unattended Compare** supplies a predetermined set of responses if you do not respond to a prompt within 15 seconds. This allows you to do a compare operation without having to be present.

- **Retry Busy Network Files** will keep trying busy network files until they become available.

- **Generate a Compare Report** will create a report of the compare operation. Useful for unattended comparisons.

- **Audible Prompts (Beep)** emits a beep when user intervention is required.

- **Quit After Compare** will quit out of Norton Backup when the comparison is complete.

Catalog   Allows you to locate a catalog stored in another drive or directory or to rebuild or retrieve one from the backup tape or diskettes. The options are the following:

- **Load** to load a different catalog file from a different directory.

- **Retrieve** to get a catalog file stored on the last disk of a backup set.

- **Rebuild** to rebuild a catalog file by scanning the diskettes in a backup set.

- **Find Files** allows you to let Norton Backup find which catalog contains the file you want to compare when you can't remember which catalog it is part of.

- **Delete** to delete a catalog file.

- **No Catalog** allows you to compare files even without a catalog. Use the Include/Exclude conditions to determine which files to compare.

To Select Files

Selecting files in the Select Compare Files window is very similar to selecting files in the Select Backup Files window. The differences are:

- No option to view files.

- No Include or Exclude options.

- A Version button, which lets you choose from multiple versions of a file if you are working from a master catalog.

● OPTIONS: ADVANCED

The Advanced program level options offer even greater flexibility in setting up file comparisons. You have all the choices from the Basic program level plus:

Select Files   Offers two additional buttons:

- **Print** which lets you print the currently selected catalog to a printer or to a file.

- **Special** which lets you limit the compare operation in the same way this button works when selecting backup files.

Options   Offers additional choices:

- **Unattended Compare** offers the same five options as in the Advanced Backup window.

- **Audible Prompts** offers the same four options as in the Advanced Backup window.

- **Network** offers the same five options as in the Advanced Backup window.

- **Reporting** offers the same five toggles as in the Advanced Backup window.

THE RESTORE WINDOW

Backing up files is fine, and it is a good idea to compare the backed-up files to the originals, but ultimately the reason for backing up files is so that you can restore them in the event of disaster. The restoration process is very similar to the comparison process and many of the options are the same. The main difference is that with Restore you are actually writing the files to your hard disk, not merely comparing them.

To Restore Files

1.   Click on the Configure button to open the Configure window.

2.   Select the program level to use. Choose OK to make the change for the current session, or Save to save the

program level permanently.

3. Click on the Restore button to switch to the Restore window. (At the Preset program level, the Compare and Restore windows are the same. Click on the Restore button to bring up the Restore window. Choose Start Restore to start the comparison.)

4. Select the backup catalog to use.

5. Select the drive to restore.

6. Select the files to restore by clicking on the Select Files button and selecting the files in the Select Restore Files window.

7. Repeat steps 5 and 6 if you have multiple drives involved in the restore operation.

8. Select from where the files are being restored.

9. If using the Basic or Advanced program level, select the location to where you want to restore the files.

10. If using the Basic or Advanced program level, click on the Options button to set any options.

11. If you're using the Basic or Advanced program level and you want to use a catalog not on the default drive and directory, or you need to rebuild or retrieve a catalog, select the Catalog button.

12. Click on the Start Restore button to begin the restore process.

PROGRAM LEVELS

The same three program levels are available as in the Backup window—Preset, Basic, and Advanced—and they are set in the Configure window.

● OPTIONS: PRESET

Backup Set Catalog   Has the names and descriptions of the master catalogs that were created when the backup sets were made. Choose the backup set you want to restore.

Select Files   Opens the Select Restore Files window, where you can select the files to restore.

Restore From   Lets you choose the location from where the backed-up files are restored.

● OPTIONS: BASIC

The Basic and Advanced restore options are very similar. The differences mirror those for the Compare operation. At the Basic program level, the options include all the options at the Preset level plus the following:

Backup Set Catalog   Lets you choose from individual catalogs or from the master catalog from each backup set.

Restore To   Lets you select the location to which to restore the backup set.

Options   Lets you choose to toggle several additional options. These are the following:

- **Verify Restore Data** compares the file on the backup disk and the file written to the hard disk. This slows the backup process but greatly improves the confidence level.

- **Perform an Unattended Restore** uses a set of predetermined responses to any prompts if they are unanswered in 15 seconds to continue the restore.

- **Retry Busy Network Files** waits for busy files when trying to restore on a Netware 286 or 386 network.

- **Generate a Restore Report** generates an ASCII report in the current catalog directory with the name *filename*.RPT, where *filename* is the name of the setup file used for the restore.

- **Prompt Before Creating Directories** asks for verification before it creates a directory.

- **Prompt Before Creating Files** asks for verification before it creates a new file that doesn't already exist on the hard disk.

- **Prompt Before Overwriting Existing Files** asks for verification before it overwrites an existing file.

- **Restore Empty Directories** creates directories that do not exist on the hard disk, even if there are no files to restore from that directory.

- **Audible Prompts (Beep)** beeps whenever an action is required on your part or an error condition occurs.

- **Quit After Restore** automatically quits when the restoration is completed.

Catalog   Lets you locate a catalog stored in another drive or directory or rebuild or retrieve one from the backup tape or diskettes. The options are the following:

- **Load** to load a different catalog file.

- **Retrieve** to get a catalog file stored on the last disk of a backup set.

- **Rebuild** to rebuild a catalog file by scanning the diskettes in a backup set.

- **Find Files** allows you to let Norton Backup find which catalog contains the file you want to compare when you can't remember which catalog it is part of.

- **Delete** to delete a catalog file.

- **No Catalog** allows you to compare files even without a catalog. Use the Include/Exclude conditions to determine which files to compare.

● OPTIONS: ADVANCED

The Advanced program level options offer even greater flexibility in setting up the Restore operation. You have all the choices from the Basic program level plus:

Select Files   Offers two additional buttons:

- **Print** which lets you print the currently selected catalog to a printer or to a file.

- **Special** which lets you limit the restore operation in the same way this button works when selecting backup files.

Options   Offers additional choices:

- **Data Verification** offers the same three choices as when using the Advanced Backup Options window.

- **Overwrite Files** offers three levels of overwrite protection. They are:

Never Overwrite Files tells Norton Backup not to restore a file if it already exists on the hard disk.

Overwrite Older Files Only tells Norton Backup to restore a file to the hard disk only if the file on the hard disk is older than the file being restored.

Always Overwrite Files tells Norton Backup to always overwrite an existing file on the hard disk, regardless of the age of the file.

- **Archive Flag** offers three different actions for the archive flag. They are:

Leave Alone which instructs Backup not to change the status of the archive flag when it restores the file.

Mark As Backed Up which causes Backup to set the archive flag off for all restored files.

Mark As NOT Backed Up which causes Backup to set the archive flag on for all restored files.

- **Network** offers the same five options as the Advanced Backup Options window.

- **Reporting** has the same five toggles as the Advanced Backup Options window.

To Select Files

Selecting files in the Select Restore Files window is the same as selecting files in the Select Compare Files window.

AUTOMATING BACKUPS

Norton Backup provides tools for creating and using automated backups to make backing up simple and fast. Automated backups can be created only at the Basic or Advanced program level, but

they can be used at any program level. You can also use the
Scheduler to begin your backup automatically.

Setup Files

Setup files contain all that is necessary to automate a backup, because they include the type of backup, file selection, backup options, and restore and compare selections and options. You can tell
Backup to use a setup file on startup by including the name of the
setup file in the command line. If you want the backup to start automatically, include **/a** (for automatic) on the command line as well.
Make sure that the setup file was made with options that will not
require operator intervention.

● EXAMPLE

To start Backup using a setup file that includes all your Quattro Pro
worksheet files, select File ➤ Run in Norton Desktop for DOS, and
assuming you have already created such a backup set and saved it
as QPRO.SET, key in the following command line:

NBACKUP.EXE QPRO.SET /A

Macros

Norton Backup includes a macro recorder that will record your keystrokes. You can use this, along with your setup files, to automate a
complicated set of backup commands or to provide other users with
the ability to select certain files while still giving them a more limited
set of options.

Macros are stored with the current setup file, and only one macro can
be stored with each setup file. You can record another macro even
though you may have one already stored with the current setup
file, but only the most recent one will be used and saved. Macros
should be recorded at the level they will be used and must begin
while in the main Norton Backup window, though they can be used
to automate backup, restore, or compare operations.

If you intend to use a macro at the Preset program level, you must
begin it at that level. Because there is no menu option for macros at
the Preset level, you will have to use the function keys to begin,

end, or insert pauses in the macro. To begin recording the macro, press F7. To insert a pause in the macro to allow the user to select files, press Alt+F7. The recording will pause until you leave the current window or dialog box and then will begin recording again. To end the macro, press F7.

At the Basic or Advanced program level, you can begin macros by selecting Macro ➤ Record or by pressing F7. To play back a macro, you must start at the main Norton Backup window, then press F8 or select Macro ➤ Run.

You can also automatically start the macro associated with a setup file from the command line by including an @ sign in front of the setup file name on the command line.

● EXAMPLE

To automatically start the macro created to go with your Quattro Pro setup file, you would use the following command line:

NBACKUP.EXE @QPRO.SET

● OPTIONS: COMMAND LINE

You can use command line options to start Norton Backup automatically, run a specific macro and setup file, and select the type of backup. You can also force Norton Backup into one of three sets of monochrome color sets, or start the restore process automatically. Norton Backup supports the following command line options:

@ Run a macro associated with the setup file

/A Immediately start the backup

/TF Do a Full Backup

/TI Do an Incremental backup

/TD Do a Differential backup

/TC Do a Full copy backup

/TO Do an Incremental copy backup

/BW Start with a black and white color set

/LCD Start with an LCD color set

/MDA Start in Monochrome Display Adapter mode

/R *[catalog filename] [restore filespec]* [/S]   Start in restore
mode, and restore files meeting the file specification from the
catalog. Include matching files in subdirectories if the /S option is included.

● **NOTE**   The @ and /A command line options are mutually
exclusive, with the @ option overriding the /A option.

NORTON DISK DOCTOR

Norton Disk Doctor (NDD) checks for and repairs errors in the system area—specifically, the partition table, boot record, directory
tree, and file allocation table (FAT)—and errors on the disk medium
itself (physically damaged sectors).

To Configure Norton Disk Doctor

1.   Select Tools ➤ Norton Disk Doctor. In the Norton Disk
Doctor dialog box, select Options.

2.   Select one of the configuration sequences below (set
surface test options, set a custom error message, or skip
certain tests).

3.   In the Disk Doctor Options dialog box, select OK to set
these options for the current session only, or select Save
Options to set options for both current and future sessions.

To Set Surface Test Options:

1.   In the Disk Doctor Options dialog box, select Surface Test.

2.   Set surface test options exactly as in steps 7 through 10 in
"To Test (and Repair) a Disk."

To Set a Custom Error Message:

1.   In the Disk Doctor Options dialog box, select Custom Message.

2. In the Set Custom Message dialog box, toggle the Prompt with Custom Message option on.

3. Press F2 to select a text attribute for the message.

4. Type the message in the message square.

5. Select OK.

Using a custom message prevents NDD from correcting system area errors (that is, errors in the FAT, directory structure, boot record, and so on) and makes steps 4, 5, and 6 in "To Test (and Repair) a Disk" unnecessary.

In step 3, there are four text attributes from which to choose: normal, bold, underline, and reverse. The text you type appears in whatever attribute is selected. You can, therefore, produce messages with multiple attributes by repeating steps 3 and 4 for different parts of the message.

To Skip Certain Tests:

1. In the Disk Doctor Options dialog box, select Tests to Skip.

2. In the Tests to Skip dialog box, select the test or tests you want to skip.

3. Select OK.

In step 2, there are four tests you can have NDD skip:

- Select Skip Partition Tests to omit testing of the integrity of the partition table on your hard disk. Some proprietary partitioning software may cause NDD difficulty.

- Select Skip CMOS Tests to omit testing of your machine's CMOS (where date, time, and configuration information is stored).

- Select Skip Surface Tests to omit testing of your disk for physical errors. Selecting this option automatically skips steps 7 through 11 in "To Test (and Repair) a Disk."

- Select Only 1 Hard Disk if your computer has only one physical hard-disk drive installed but NDD reports more than one.

To Quit NDD

- In the Norton Disk Doctor dialog box, select Quit Disk Doctor or press Esc.

To Test (and Repair) a Disk

1. In the Norton Disk Doctor dialog box, select Diagnose Disk.

2. In the Select Drives to Diagnose dialog box, select the disk or disks you want to test, and then select Diagnose.

3. If errors are found, read the explanation box(es) and select Continue.

4. When prompted to correct errors, select Yes to correct them or No to let them alone.

5. Follow any prompts NDD presents to correct errors.

6. In the Create UNDO File dialog box, select the drive on which you want to store the Undo file, or select Skip Undo File to skip this step.

7. In the Surface Test dialog box and in the Test box, select whether you want NDD to test the entire surface of the disk for damage or just the space occupied by files.

8. In the Test Type box, select the surface test depth (how thoroughly NDD tests the disk surface).

9. In the Passes box, select how many times you want NDD to perform the surface test.

10. In the Repair Setting box, select a repair option.

11. Select Begin Test.

12. On the summary screen, optionally print a report of NDD findings and actions by selecting Report.

13. On the Report for Drive screen, select Print to print the NDD report, or select Save as to save it in a file. If you choose Save as, enter the name of the report file in the Save Report dialog box.

14. Select Done.

In step 2, select the drives you want to diagnose by highlighting them and pressing the spacebar or by clicking on them once with the mouse.

If you select No in step 4, NDD does not correct the errors it has found, and you skip to step 7.

In step 5, the actual dialog boxes you see depend on the errors found.

In step 6, you create a file that allows you to undo NDD's corrections. (See "To Undo NDD Corrections.")

Steps 7 through 11 constitute the surface test, which checks for physical errors on a disk. If you want to skip these steps, select Cancel in step 7 and go to step 12. Otherwise, in step 7, select Disk Test to have NDD test the entire disk surface for physical errors, or select File Test to have it test only the areas of the disk with data (files) on them.

In step 8, there are three types of tests:

- Select Daily to have NDD perform a "light" test.

- Select Weekly to have NDD perform a more thorough (and longer) test.

- Select Auto Weekly (the default) if you are going to use NDD every day for preventive maintenance. This option causes NDD to perform a Daily test on every day of the week (as determined by your system clock) except Friday, when it performs a Weekly test.

In step 9, select Repetitions to specify exactly how many times the surface test is to be done. Select Continuous to run the surface test until you interrupt it.

In step 10, you set the repair options for the surface test, not the system area test that occurs in steps 2 through 5.

- Select Don't Repair if you want to leave any surface errors NDD finds.

- Select Prompt before Repairing to have NDD prompt you before it fixes a surface error.

- Select Repair Automatically to have NDD fix any errors it finds without prompting you first.

To Undo NDD Corrections

1. In the Norton Disk Doctor dialog box, select Undo Changes.
2. In the Undo Changes dialog box, select Yes.
3. Select the drive containing the Undo file.
4. Select OK in the confirmation box.
5. Select OK to acknowledge completion of the operation.

This function allows you to undo the changes or corrections made with NDD. To undo NDD corrections, however, you must have saved an Undo file in step 6 of "To Test (and Repair) a Disk."

The Undo file is always called NDDUNDO.DAT.

● SYNTAX

NDD [*drive*:] [*drive*:] [/*options*]

drive: specifies the drive(s) to test and repair.

The options are the following:

/C   Tests the system area and performs a surface test on the indicated drive(s).

/Q   Tests the system area but does not perform a surface test.

/DT   Performs only the surface test.

/R:*filename*   Sends a report to the specified file. Use this option with /Q, /C, or /DT.

/RA:*filename*   Appends a report to the specified file. Use this option with /Q, /C, or /DT.

/REBUILD   Has NDD attempt to reconstruct a critically damaged disk.

/UNDELETE   Undeletes a partition.

/X:*drive*   Excludes the specified drive from testing. Excluded drives do not appear for selection in the Select Drives to Diagnose dialog box.

/SKIPHIGH   Avoids using high memory.

SCHEDULER

The Scheduler allows you to run programs and display messages at preset times. To run events, the Scheduler terminate-and-stay-resident (TSR) program must be loaded. The best way to do this is to have the Scheduler/Screen Saver as one of your startup programs. (See "Startup Programs" in Part Two.) You can also type **NSCHED** at the DOS prompt to install Scheduler. If your computer is turned on and Scheduler is installed, the events you schedule will be performed regardless of what else you happen to be doing at the time.

To Configure Scheduler

1.   Select Tools ➤ Scheduler.

2.   Click on the List button. In the Event List Options dialog box, select the type of Event List you want. Monthly lists all events for the highlighted month. Daily lists events for the highlighted day. All Events lists everything currently scheduled. Select whether you want a one- or two-line display for your events. Click on OK.

To View a List of Scheduled Events

1.   Select the day you want displayed by using the mouse or the cursor direction keys.

2.   Select the month you want displayed by clicking on the right and left arrowheads on the month title bar. Or use the PgUp and PgDn keys.

To Add an Event to Scheduler

1.   Select Tools ➤ Scheduler.

2.   Click on the Add button to see the Event Editor dialog box.

3.   Select the Event Type first. This will determine which options are available and which are dimmed-out.

4.   Fill in the date and time for the event. For a repeating event, enter the first date on which it should run. Choose Frequency from the choices in the drop-down list. If your choice is Weekly, choose the Day of Week from the drop-down list. Select the Custom button to choose a frequency of more than once a week but not daily or weekdays.

5.   For a program or batch file, choose a time for a confirmation delay. Certain events can take over your computer for an extended period. If you choose a time other than No Delay, a confirmation box will appear when the event is scheduled. You can then choose to proceed, cancel the event, or postpone it. The amount of time in the Confirmation Delay box is the amount of time the program will wait before continuing.

6.   Key in a description of the event in the Description box. This is the text that will appear on the events list.

7.   Type in the path and executable file name on the Command line, or select the Browse button to help you locate the file you want. In the case of a Reminder, type in the message you want to appear, up to 160 characters long.

8.   Click on OK to save your event. Select OK in Scheduler to exit.

To Create a Batch File

1.   Select Batch File as the Event Type in the Event Editor.

2.   Type in the name of the batch file on the Command line. Click on the Edit button. A box opens with the message This batch file does not exist. Do you want to create it? Select OK.

3. In the Batch File Editor, type in the text of the batch file.

4. Select Save when you are finished. Select OK in the Event Editor to add the new event.

To later edit a batch file, click on the Add button. Select Batch File from the Event Type drop-down list. Type in the name of the batch file on the Command line and click on Edit. The Batch File Editor opens with the selected batch file displayed. Click on Save when finished to save your changes.

If the batch file is associated with a currently scheduled event, highlight it in the Events list and click on Edit. Proceed as above.

To Edit or Remove Events

1. Open the Scheduler and highlight an event.

2. Click on Edit to modify the details of an event. Click on Delete to delete the event from the list.

● **NOTE** In order to protect your data, Scheduler must be disabled while certain Norton Utilities are running. The programs that disable Scheduler are:

- Disk Tools
- Image
- Norton Disk Doctor
- Norton Mail
- Speed Disk
- UnErase
- UnFormat

Scheduler is also disabled while you are using Disk ➤ Format Diskette.

These programs will only delay a scheduled event until you exit the program. A message will then appear on your desktop asking if you want to run it now.

SPEED DISK

When DOS writes a file to disk, the first cluster in the file is placed in the first available cluster on the disk, the next cluster in the file is placed in the next available cluster, and so on, filling the disk from front to back. As a result, when files are copied onto an empty hard disk, each file's clusters sit together in one area of the disk.

After much use, however, a file's clusters can be scattered over different areas of the disk. For example, if a 20K file is deleted and a 25K file is written to the disk, the first 20K of the new file fits into the vacated space, while the remaining 5K must be placed elsewhere. Although this is simply a result of normal DOS bookkeeping, a hard disk with files scattered all over will noticeably slow down your computer. The read-write heads must travel the entire surface of the disk just to find one file.

Finding a file is much faster if its component clusters are consecutive. Speed Disk optimizes, or defragments, your hard disk, placing the clusters of each file next to one another and moving all files toward the beginning of the disk.

To Defragment/Optimize a Hard Disk

1. Select Tools ➤ Speed Disk.

2. In the dialog box that appears, select the drive you want to defragment.

3. In the Recommendation dialog box, select Optimize to run Speed Disk as it is currently configured, or select Configure to reconfigure the program. If you select Optimize, skip to step 12. If you select Configure, continue with steps 4 through 11.

4. Optionally specify the order in which directories are written to disk during optimization. (See "To Specify Directory Order.")

5. Optionally specify the order in which files are to be listed within directories. (See "To Specify File Sort Order.")

6. Optionally specify files that should be placed at the beginning of the disk during optimization. (See "To Place Files at the Beginning of a Disk.")

7. Optionally specify files that are not to be moved during optimization. (See "To Specify Unmovable Files.")

8. Optionally set miscellaneous options. (See "To Set Miscellaneous Speed Disk Options.")

9. Optionally specify the method of optimization. (See "To Select an Optimization Method.")

10. Save the new configuration. Pull down the Configure menu, and select the Save Options to Disk option.

11. Pull down the Optimize menu and select the Begin optimization option, or press Alt+B. The optimization process may take some time to finish.

12. Select OK to acknowledge completion of the operation.

13. In the dialog box that appears, select Another Drive to defragment another drive, select Configure to change program configuration, or select Exit to DOS if you are finished. If you select Another Drive, go back to step 2. If you select Configure, go back to step 4.

To Place Files at the Beginning of a Disk

1. Pull down the Configure menu, and select the Files to Place First option.

2. In the Files to Place First dialog box, optionally add a file specification to the file list. Select Insert and type an additional specification to add to the top of the list. Use the ↓ to add to the bottom of the list. Repeat as necessary.

3. Optionally remove a file specification from the file list by highlighting the file specification and selecting Delete. Repeat as necessary.

4. Optionally rearrange the order of the files. Highlight a file specification you want to relocate, select Move to tag it,

use ↑ and ↓ or the mouse to relocate it, and select Move
again to untag it. Repeat as necessary.

5.   Select OK.

As a general rule, you get an increase in hard-disk performance if
frequently accessed files (those that will not change in size, such as
.COM or .EXE files) are placed at the beginning of the disk, thus
minimizing the distance the read-write heads must go to find them.
This function allows you to specify the files to be placed at the
beginning of the disk.

To Quit Speed Disk

- Select Exit from the Optimize menu, or press Esc.

To Save the Current Configuration

- Pull down the Configure menu, and select the Save
  Options to Disk option.

Saved settings remain in effect in the current session and in future
sessions until they are changed again.

To Select a Different
Drive to Defragment/Optimize

1.   Pull down the Optimize menu, and select the Drive option.

2.   In the dialog box that appears, select the drive to defragment or optimize.

3.   Go to step 3 in "To Defragment/Optimize a Hard Disk."

Use this function if, during configuration (steps 4 through 10), you
want to defragment or optimize a different drive from the one
you initially chose.

To Select an Optimization Method

1.   Pull down the Optimize menu, and select the Optimization Method option.

2.   In the Select Optimization Method dialog box, select from five available options:

- **Full Optimization** defragments all files and moves them toward the beginning of the disk, closing all gaps.

- **Full with Directories First** defragments all files, closes all gaps, and moves directories to the very beginning of the disk.

- **Full with File Reorder** defragments all files, closes all gaps, moves directories to the very beginning of the disk, and sorts files. This is the most comprehensive optimization option.

- **Unfragment Files Only** defragments all files but does not close gaps.

- **Unfragment Free Space** fills empty space by moving files toward the beginning of the disk without unfragmenting them.

3.   Select OK.

In step 2, select Full Optimization to defragment all files without directory and file reordering. If you select Unfragment Files Only, each file's clusters will be placed consecutively on the disk, but files won't be moved toward the beginning of the disk. This option is faster than Full Optimization but not as thorough, because it can leave empty space between files.

Select Unfragment Free Space to move data forward to the beginning of the disk. This option does not defragment files but only fills empty space. Though faster than both of the previous options, it is not as effective. Select Full with Directories First to optimize the disk plus move directories to the front of the disk. Select Full with File Reorder to optimize the disk and sort your files as they are listed in their directories. To specify the order in which files are listed, see "To Specify File Sort Order."

To Set Miscellaneous Speed Disk Options

1.   Pull down the Configure menu, and select Other Options.

2.   Toggle any of three available options:

- **Read-After-Write** checks that data was properly writtten to a new location on disk.

- **Clear Unused Space** overwrites all unused space as data is relocated.

- **Beep When Done** enables or disables beep upon completion of optimization.

3.   Select OK.

To Specify Directory Order

1.   Pull down the Configure menu, and select the Directory Order option.

2.   In the Select Directory Order dialog box, optionally highlight a directory in the Directory list box and select Add to add it to the Directory Order box. Repeat as necessary.

3.   Optionally highlight a directory in the Directory Order box, and select Delete to remove it. Repeat as necessary.

4.   Optionally rearrange files in the Directory Order box. Highlight the directory you want to relocate, select Move to tag it, use ↑ and ↓ or the mouse to reposition the directory, and select Move again to untag it. Repeat as necessary.

5.   Select OK.

Use this function to specify the order in which directories are written on the disk during Full Optimization or Directory Optimization. (See "To Select an Optimization Method.") As a general rule, the best performance results from placing the most frequently accessed directories first. Directories are placed as they are listed in the Directory Order box in the Select Directory Order dialog box.

In step 2, you can move the highlight quickly by using built-in Speed Search. To use Speed Search, simply type the first letter or letters of the directory you want to highlight. Each time you type a letter, the highlight bar jumps to the next directory name beginning with the letters typed. Pressing Ctrl+Enter cycles the highlight bar through all directories that match the current search string.

In step 4, some rearranging is usually necessary, because directories added to the Directory Order box are placed at the top of the list.

To Specify File Sort Order

1. Pull down the Configure menu, and select the File Sort option. The File Sort dialog box appears.

2. In the Sort Criterion box, select how files are to be sorted.

3. In the Sort Order box, specify whether files are to be sorted in Ascending or Descending order.

4. Select OK.

Use this function to specify the order in which files will be listed in their directories. This sorting can be accomplished by a file sort or by any kind of optimization. (See "To Select an Optimization Method.")

In step 2, there are five options from which to choose:

- **Unsorted** to leave files in whatever order they may be in
- **Name** to sort files by file name
- **Extension** to sort files by file extension
- **Date & Time** to sort files by file date and time
- **Size** to sort files in order of their size

In step 3, the Ascending and Descending options have no effect if the sort order is set to Unsorted in step 2.

To Specify Unmovable Files

1. Pull down the Configure menu, and select the Unmovable Files option.

2. In the Unmovable Files dialog box, type the complete name of a file that is not to be moved and press ↓. Repeat as necessary.

3. Optionally remove files from the list by highlighting them and selecting Delete.

4. Select OK when finished.

Some files, such as those employed by certain copy-protection schemes, should not be repositioned on the disk. Speed Disk is good at identifying such files. This function allows for manual editing of the unmovable file list.

To View a File Fragmentation Report

1. Pull down the Information menu, and select the Fragmentation Report option.

2. In the directory tree in the File Fragmentation Report dialog box, highlight a directory whose files you want to detail. Repeat as necessary.

3. Select OK when finished.

In step 2, you can move the highlight quickly by using built-in Speed Search. To use Speed Search, simply type the first letter or letters of the directory you want to highlight. Each time you type a letter, the highlight bar jumps to the next directory name beginning with the letters typed. Pressing Ctrl+Enter cycles the highlight bar through all directories that match the current search string.

The report details the name of each file in the highlighted directory, the percentage of the file that is unfragmented, the total number of fragments that make up the file, and the number of clusters the file occupies.

Files that are moderately fragmented (90 percent or more) are shown in a contrasting color (usually red) on a color display and are bulleted on a monochrome display. Files that are highly fragmented (89 percent or less) are shown in another contrasting color (usually magenta) on a color display and are bulleted on a monochrome display. Files that are 100 percent unfragmented are displayed normally.

To View the Map Legend

1.   Pull down the Information menu, and select the Map
Legend option.

2.   Select OK when you are finished reading.

A partial legend appears on the screen with the disk map. Use this
option to display a complete legend.

To View Relevant Disk Information

1.   Pull down the Information menu, and select the Disk
Statistics option.

2.   Select OK when you are finished reading.

This function provides such information as disk size, percentage of
disk space that is occupied and free, number of files on the disk,
number of clusters allocated to files and directories, and number of
unused clusters.

To View a Static File List

1.   Pull down the Information menu, and select the Show
static files option.

2.   Select OK when finished.

This function lists files deemed unmovable by Speed Disk, as well
as those specified as unmovable by the user. (See "To Specify Unmovable Files.")

To Walk the Disk Map

1.   Pull down the Information menu, and select the Walk map
option.

2.   Move the flashing block to the cluster whose contents you
want to detail, and press Enter.

3. Select OK when you're finished reading the Contents of Map Block dialog box.

4. Repeat steps 2 and 3 as necessary.

This function details the contents of cluster blocks as they appear on the Speed Disk disk map. Specifically, it shows which clusters are represented by the block, which files belong to the clusters, and whether the clusters are optimized or fragmented.

In step 2, you can move the flashing block with the mouse or the cursor keys. When using the mouse, drag the flashing block or simply click on the target cluster. When using the arrow keys, press Enter to detail the target cluster.

After step 3, you can detail other blocks. When finished, if you have been using the arrow keys and the flashing block is still visible, press the Escape key. If you have been using the mouse, simply select the next function you want to perform.

● SYNTAX

SPEEDISK [*drive:*] [*/options*]

drive: specifies the drive to defragment/optimize. If you specify a drive on the command line, omit step 2 in "To Defragment/Optimize a Hard Disk."

The options are the following:

/B   Reboots the computer after defragmentation/optimization.

/F   Specifies a full disk optimization. (See "To Select an Optimization Method.")

/FD   Specifies a full optimization with directories first. (See "To Select an Optimization Method.")

/FF   Specifies Full with File Reorder optimization. (See "To Select an Optimization Method.")

/Q   Specifies Unfragment Free Space. (See "To Select an Optimization Method.")

/SD[-]   Sorts files by date and time. Append the optional hyphen to sort in descending order.

/SE[-]   Sorts files by extension. Append the optional hyphen to sort in descending order.

/SN[-]   Sorts files by file name. Append the optional hyphen to sort in descending order.

/SS[-]   Sorts files by file size. Append the optional hyphen to sort in descending order.

/U   Specifies Unfragment Files Only. (See "To Select an Optimization Method.")

/V   Toggles the Read-After-Write option on. (See "To Set Miscellaneous Speed Disk Options.")

/SKIPHIGH   Prevents loading of data in high memory.

SYSTEM INFORMATION

System Information provides screens of information about most aspects of your computer. It details system configuration, gives complete characteristics of installed drives, details memory usage, and provides CPU and hard-disk benchmarks.

To Cycle through Information Screens Consecutively

- At the bottom of any information screen, select Next to see the next screen in sequence. Select Previous to see the previous one.

The order in which information screens appear corresponds to the order of options on the pull-down menus. The first screen (System Summary) is the first option on the first menu, the second screen is the second option, and so on.

To Print a Complete System Summary Report

1.   Pull down the Report menu, and select Print report.

2. In the Report Options dialog box, select the information screens you want to include in the report.

3. In the User Text box, optionally toggle the Report header option to include a header in the report.

4. Optionally toggle the Notes at end of report option to append comments at the end of the report.

5. Select the Printer button to send the report to your printer. Select File to send the report to a file.

6. If you are printing to a file, type the path and file name to which you want output sent, and select OK.

7. If you are printing to a file, select OK to acknowledge completion. If either the Report Header or Notes at End of Report option is on, you will be prompted to enter the text you want. Select OK when finished.

This function allows you to print the contents of multiple information screens in one report. The Report Options dialog box has an option for every information screen in System Information.

Comments in the User Notes dialog box can occupy a maximum of ten lines. Move the cursor between lines by using ↑ and ↓ only. Pressing Enter terminates input and is equivalent to selecting OK.

To Print an Information Screen

1. Select the Print button at the bottom of the information screen.

2. In the Print Current Information dialog box, select Printer to send the output to your printer. Select File to send output to a file.

3. If you are printing to a file, type the path and file name to which you want output sent, and select OK.

4. Select OK to acknowledge completion.

To Quit System Information

• Select System ➤ Exit, or press Esc twice.

To View a Particular Information Screen

Each information screen can be accessed by selecting one option on one menu. The screens show the following information:

- **System Summary:** type of main processor, math coprocessor, BIOS, video standard, mouse, keyboard, bus, amount of memory installed, number and types of drives, number of ports, and type of operating system running.

- **Video Summary:** kind of card installed, kind of monitor installed, current video mode, character size, maximum number of on-screen scan lines, amount of video memory, video page size, and address of first segment of video memory.

- **Hardware Interrupts:** hardware interrupt usage.

- **Software Interrupts:** software interrupt usage.

- **Network Information:** current user and type of network.

- **CMOS Status:** status and contents of CMOS, including type and number of installed drives and amount and kind of memory installed.

- **Disk Summary:** number of drives installed, drive letters assigned to them, and their type, capacity, and current default directory.

- **Disk Characteristics:** logical and physical characteristics of any drive on your system (select the drive in the drive list box in the upper-right corner of the Disk Characteristics screen).

- **Partition Tables:** location and contents of partition table.

- **Memory Usage Summary:** kind and amount of memory installed, how much is used, and how much is free.

- **Expanded Memory (EMS):** display of technical information about any expanded memory (amount used and available), LIM driver version, and so on.

- **Extended Memory (XMS):** display of technical information about any extended memory (amount used and available) driver version, and so on.

- **Memory Block List:** details on first 640K of memory, listing what applications are loaded, the starting address and size of each application, and to what memory block each belongs.

- **TSR Programs:** name, location in memory, and size of TSRs loaded.

- **Device Drivers:** devices loaded, the starting memory address, and description of each.

- **CPU Speed:** speed of CPU relative to Compaq 386/33, IBM PC/AT (8 MHz), and IBM PC/XT (4.77 MHz).

- **Hard Disk Speed:** speed of hard disk relative to hard disks that come standard with Compaq 386/33, IBM PC/AT (8 MHz), and IBM PC/XT (4.77 MHz); average access times commonly used for comparing hard disks.

- **Overall Performance Index:** combination of CPU speed and hard-disk speed tests, comparing overall speed with Compaq 386/33, IBM PC/AT (8 MHz), and IBM PC/XT (4.77 MHz).

- **Network Performance Speed:** read and write tests of network server's hard disk, measuring throughput in kilobytes per second.

- **View CONFIG.SYS File:** display of CONFIG.SYS file.

- **View AUTOEXEC.BAT File:** display of AUTOEXEC.BAT file.

● **SYNTAX**

SYSINFO [*drive:*] [*/options*]

The options are the following:

/AUTO: #   Cycles continuously through all information screens at intervals of # seconds. Press Esc to stop and return to DOS.

/DEMO   Cycles continuously through the System Summary screen and Benchmark screens at 5-second intervals. Press Esc to stop and return to DOS.

/DI   Displays a summary screen of drive information only.

drive: Specifies the drive on which information is wanted (if omitted, default drive).

/N   Starts System Information without memory scan.

/SOUND   Sounds a beep after each test of the CPU when you run the Benchmarks CPU Speed option.

/SUMMARY   Displays the System Summary screen without loading the System Information program shell.

/TSR   Displays a list of loaded TSRs.

UNERASE

UnErase enables you to recover all or parts of erased files. When a file is erased, its entry is removed from the directory structure and the FAT (file allocation table). The file's data, however, remains on the disk, making unerasure possible. If an erased file's data is not overwritten by another file that uses the same disk space, UnErase can recover the erased file in its entirety. If erased data is partially overwritten, UnErase allows you to reassemble the remaining parts manually.

To Add Data to an Existing File

1.   Highlight the file to which you want to add data.

2.   Pull down the File menu, and select the Append To option.

3.   Go to step 4 in "To UnErase a File Manually."

This function allows you to add clusters manually to a file that already exists or has been unerased. It is only available if you highlight an existing file. Therefore, you may have to toggle the Include Non-Erased Files option on. To find out how to do this, see "To Include Existing Files on the File List."

To Change the Current Directory

1. Pull down the File menu and select the Change Directory
option, or press Alt+R.

2. In the Change Directory dialog box, highlight the directory to which you want to change, and select OK.

In step 2, you can move the highlight quickly by using built-in
Speed Search. To use Speed Search, simply type the first letter or
letters of the directory you want to highlight. Each time you type a
letter, the highlight bar jumps to the next directory name beginning
with the letters typed. Pressing Ctrl+Enter cycles the highlight bar
through all directories that match the current search string.

Because directories always appear on the file list, some directory
navigation is also possible from the file list itself. Double-clicking or
pressing Enter when a directory is highlighted makes that directory
the current one.

To Change the Current Drive

1. Pull down the File menu and select the Change Drive
option, or press Alt+D.

2. In the Change Drive dialog box, select a drive.

To Include Existing Files on the File List

• Pull down the Options menu, and select the Include Non-
Erased Files option.

This option is a toggle. When toggled on, both erased and existing
files appear on the file list. When toggled off, only erased files appear. This option is not available when the file list displays the
results of a search (see "To Search for Erased Files in Erased Directories," "To Search Erased Disk Space for Specific Text," and "To
Search for Deleted Data Fragments").

To List All Files on the Current Drive

- Pull down the File menu and select the View All Directories option, or press Alt+A.

Use this function to display all files on the current drive. You can list all files or only erased files (see "To Include Existing Files on the File List").

To List Files in the Current Directory Only

- Pull down the File menu and select the View Current Directory option, or press Alt+C.

Use this function to display only the current directory on the file list. You can list all files or only erased files (see "To Include Existing Files on the File List").

To Quit UnErase

- Select File ➤ Exit or press Esc.

To Rename a File

1. Highlight the file you want to rename.
2. Pull down the File menu, and select the Rename option.
3. In the Rename dialog box, type the new file name and select OK.

This function is only available if the highlighted file already exists or has been recovered. (See "To Include Existing Files on the File List" if you want existing files on the file list.) It is not available if any files have been tagged.

To Resume a Discontinued Search

- Pull down the Search menu, and select the Continue Search option.

Use this function to resume a search (for lost names, text, or data types) that you have interrupted.

To Search for Deleted Data Fragments

1. Pull down the Search menu, and select the For Data Types option.

2. In the Search for Data Types dialog box, select the data types for which you want to search.

3. Select OK.

This function searches the erased portion of the disk for specific kinds of data. In step 2, select one of the following options:

- **Normal Text** to search for ASCII text

- **Lotus 1-2-3 and Symphony** to search for Lotus and compatible spreadsheet data

- **dBASE** to search for database data

- **Other Data** to search for anything else

When a match is found, the cluster or clusters containing the search string are given a file name and appear on the file list, available for unerasure (see "To UnErase a File or Group of Files Automatically"). File names begin with FILE0000; subsequent file names are numbered sequentially. The appended extensions depend on the kind of data contained in the file. Text files have the .TXT extension, database files have .DBF, spreadsheet files have .WK1, and all others have .DAT.

To Search Erased Disk Space for Specific Text

1. Pull down the Search menu, and select the For Text option.

2. In the Search for Text dialog box, type the string for which you want to search.

3. Optionally toggle the Ignore Case option off for a case-sensitive search.

4. Select OK.

This function searches erased disk space for text you specify. When a match is found, the cluster or clusters containing the search string are given a file name and appear on the file list, available for unerasure (see "To UnErase a File or Group of Files Automatically"). File names begin with FILE0000; subsequent file names are numbered sequentially.

In step 3, the Ignore Case switch toggles case-sensitive searches on or off. If it is turned on (the default), then the search is not case-sensitive. Searching for *Alfie* will find every consecutive occurrence of the letters *a-l-f-i-e* without regard to case. If it is turned off, then the search will only find exact matches of the search string. Searching for *Alfie* will only find *Alfie*, and not *ALFIE, alfie, alFie,* and so on.

To Search for Erased
Files in Erased Directories

- Pull down the Search menu, and select the For Lost Names option.

The names of erased files are kept in existing directories and are listed for unerasure on the file list. When a directory is deleted, however, the names of deleted files contained in the directory cannot be so easily accessed. This function searches the disk for the names of erased files in erased directories—lost names. When found, the lost files can be unerased, completely or partially, depending on how much of their data has been overwritten (see "To UnErase a File or Group of Files Automatically" and "To UnErase a File Manually").

To Sort the File List

1.   Pull down the Options menu.

2.   Select one of the six available sort options.

In step 2, select one of the following options:

- **Sort by Name** to sort the file list by name
- **Sort by Extension** to sort by file extension

- **Sort by Time** to sort by file date and time—only available when viewing files in the current directory (see "To List Files in the Current Directory Only")

- **Sort by Size** to sort by file size

- **Sort by Directory** to sort alphabetically by directory—available when viewing all files on the current drive (see "To List All Files on the Current Drive")

- **Sort by Prognosis** to sort by prognosis for successful recovery

To Specify the Range of a Search

1. Pull down the Search menu, and select the Set Search Range option.

2. In the Search Range dialog box and at the Starting Cluster prompt, type the number of the first cluster of the range you want to search.

3. At the Ending Cluster prompt, type the number of the last cluster in the range you want to search.

4. Select OK.

When you start a search, UnErase, by default, searches the entire current disk. Use this function if you want to limit searches to particular parts of the current disk.

To Tag a File for Unerasure

1. Highlight the file you want to tag.

2. Pull down the File menu and select the Select option, or press the spacebar, or click the right mouse button.

The Select option is only available when an untagged file is highlighted.

To Tag a Group of Files for Unerasure

1. Pull down the File menu and select the Select Group op-
    tion or press the gray plus key on the numeric keypad.

2. In the Select dialog box, type a file specification for the
    files you want to tag (*.TXT, *.DOC, *.*, and so on), and
    select OK.

To UnErase a File or
Group of Files Automatically

1. Highlight or tag the file(s) you want to unerase.

2. Select the UnErase button.

3. In the UnErase dialog box, optionally toggle the Prompt
    for Missing 1st Letters option off and select UnErase.

4. Enter the first letter of the file name.

UnErase makes the automatic unerasure of files simple and straight-
forward. It is merely a matter of manipulating the file list to show
the file you want to unerase.

In step 1, see "To Tag a File for Unerasure" and "To Tag a Group of
Files for Unerasure" if necessary.

In step 3, an erased file loses the first letter of its file name. When
unerasing a file, therefore, the first letter of the file name must be
supplied. Toggle the Prompt for Missing 1st Letters option off if
you do not want to supply the first letter for each file. This causes
UnErase to make *a* the first letter of each unerased file. Omit step 3
if you are unerasing only one highlighted file, that is, if you have
not actually tagged any files.

Omit step 4 if the Prompt for Missing 1st Letters option is toggled
off in step 3.

To UnErase a File Manually

1. Highlight the file you want to unerase.

2. Pull down the File menu and select the Manual UnErase option, or press Alt+M.

3. In the UnErase dialog box, enter the first letter of the erased file's name.

4. In the Manual Unerase dialog box, select Add Cluster.

5. In the Add Clusters dialog box, select one of the four options for adding a cluster or group of clusters to the file.

6. Optionally select View File to see the contents of the clusters assembled so far. Select OK in the View File dialog box when you're finished.

7. Optionally select View Map to see the area(s) on the disk map used by the assembled clusters. Select OK in the View Map dialog box when you're finished.

8. Repeat steps 4 through 7 as necessary.

9. Select Save to save the unerased file.

Unerasing a file manually requires that you assemble (steps 4 and 5) and save (step 9) a file's component clusters. So that you can keep track, all assembled clusters are listed by number in the Added Clusters box in the Manual UnErase dialog box. You can unerase only one file at a time, even if more than one file on the file list is tagged.

In step 5, select one of the following options:

- **All clusters** to have UnErase assemble all the clusters likely to belong to the file

- **Next probable** to have UnErase add only the next most probable cluster

- **Data search** to add clusters by searching for specific data

- **Cluster number** to assemble a specific cluster or range of clusters

If you select Data Search, follow these steps before going to step 6:

- In the Data Search dialog box, enter a search string in ASCII characters at the ASCII prompt or in hex characters at the Hex prompt.

- Optionally toggle the Ignore Case option off for a case-sensitive search.

- Select Find.

- When a match is found, it appears in the View File dialog box. Select Hex to view the data as hex characters or Text to view the data as ASCII characters.

- Select Add Cluster if you want to add the cluster containing the match to the list of assembled clusters.

- Select Find Next to search for the next occurrence of the search string.

- Repeat the fourth, fifth, and sixth steps if necessary.

- Select Done when you are finished searching and have gathered the clusters you want to add to the file.

If you select Cluster Number, follow these steps before going to step 6:

- In the Add Cluster Number dialog box and at the Starting Cluster prompt, type the number of the first cluster in the range of clusters you want to add to the file.

- At the Ending Cluster prompt, type the name of the last cluster in the range of clusters.

- Select OK.

In step 9, the clusters you have assembled or added will be recovered as one file. If, however, the clusters you have assembled are, taken together, smaller than the original file, there is one extra step: In the Confirm Save dialog box, select Save Anyway to save what you have, or select Resume to go back to step 4.

To UnErase a File to a New File Name Manually

1. Highlight the file you want to unerase.
2. Pull down the File menu and select the Create File option.

3. In the UnErase dialog box, type the new file name and select OK.

4. Go to step 4 in "To Unerase a File Manually."

This function allows you to erase a file manually and to give the file a name different from its original name.

To Unerase a File to a New Location Automatically

1. Highlight the file you want to unerase.

2. Pull down the File menu, and select the UnErase To option.

3. In the UnErase To dialog box, select a new drive for the unerased file.

4. Edit the suggested path and file name as needed, and select OK.

In step 4, you have to edit the suggested path if you want to place the unerased file in a subdirectory of the drive you specified in step 3, or if you want to supply the correct first letter of the file name. Erased files lose the first letter of the file name, so UnErase may automatically attach an *a* during this procedure (not necessarily, if SmartCan is running).

To Untag a Group of Files

1. Pull down the File menu and select the Unselect Group option or press the gray minus key on the numeric keypad.

2. In the Unselect dialog box, type the file specification for the files you want to untag (*.DOC, *.*, and so on), and select OK.

The Unselect Group option is only available when one or more files are tagged.

To Untag a Single File

1. Highlight the tagged file you want to untag.

2. Pull down the File menu and select the Unselect option, or press the spacebar, or click the right mouse button.

The Unselect option is only available when a tagged file is highlighted.

To View the Contents of a File on the File List

1. Highlight the file whose contents you want to view.

2. Select the View button.

3. In the View File dialog box, select OK when finished.

In step 3, the View File dialog box has other options. If the file is presented in text mode, select Hex to view the file in hex characters. If the file is presented in hex mode, select Text to view the file in ASCII characters. Select Next to view the next file on the file list, and select Prev to view the previous file on the file list.

To View Pertinent Information about a File on the File List

1. Highlight the file about which you want information.

2. Select the Info button.

3. In the Information dialog box, select OK when finished.

This function shows the erased file's name, date, time, size, attributes, prognosis for unerasure, the number of its starting cluster, and the number of clusters that comprise the file.

In step 3, the Information dialog box has two other options. Select Next to view information about the next file on the file list. Select Prev to view information about the previous file.

● **SYNTAX**

UNERASE [*filespec*] [/IMAGE] [/MIRROR] [/NOTRACK] [/SKIPHIGH] [/SMARTCAN] [/NOSMARTCAN]

The options are the following:

filespec   Specifies the name of the file or group of files you want to unerase. If *filespec* is just a file name, *filespec* is unerased automatically, and the program returns you to the DOS prompt. If, however, *filespec* uses wildcards, the UnErase program comes up with all files matching *filespec* tagged. You must then take appropriate steps to unerase these files. (See "To UnErase a File or Group of Files Automatically" and "To UnErase a File Manually.")

/IMAGE   Use the Image recovery information (excludes MIRROR).

/MIRROR   Use the Mirror recovery information (excludes IMAGE).

/NOTRACK   Exclude Delete tracking information.

/SKIPHIGH   Do not use High Memory.

/SMARTCAN   Unerase only files saved by SmartCan.

/NOSMARTCAN   Exclude files saved by SmartCan.

Part Five

Standalone Programs

ADVISE

Advise is a very useful program that will help you diagnose common disk problems and interpret error messages from DOS. Advise then provides recommended courses of action.

To Open Advise

1. Select Help ➤ Advise.

2. The Advise main index is displayed. The first two entries, "What is Advise" and "How to Use Advise," are help screens for Advise. The next three entries are the problem groups.

3. Highlight the entry you want and select the Go To button, or double-click on the entry. Use the Index button to return to the main index screen at any point.

To Select an Advise Topic

1. Open Advise. From the main index screen, select the topic you want. Double-click on it or select the Go To button.

2. Double-click on the error message or highlight it and select Go To. The explanation screen will open. This screen explains the topic and recommends a course of action.

3. In the explanation screen, some terms will be displayed in a contrasting color. If it is a technical term, double-clicking on it will open a screen with a definition. If it is a Norton Desktop for DOS program, double-clicking will exit Advise and start the specified program.

● **NOTE**   Occasionally, the problem cannot be corrected by Norton Desktop for DOS—for example, if your hard disk is so damaged that DOS cannot read it. However, if you have Norton Utilities, Advise will run the correct program for you.

DISK TOOLS

Disk Tools is a collection of five functions that can fix problems ranging from the fairly common to the catastrophic. Specifically, you can make a nonbootable disk bootable, restore the damage done by the DOS RECOVER program, reformat an error-laden disk without loss of data, save critical system information on a separate disk, and restore that information, if needed.

To Create a Rescue Disk

1. Start Disk Tools.

2. Highlight Create Rescue Diskette on the Procedures list.

3. Select Proceed.

4. Select OK after you read the information screen.

5. Select the disk on which you will store rescue information. Insert a disk in the indicated drive.

6. When the operation is complete, select OK to return to the Disk Tools main screen.

Create Rescue Diskette stores vital disk information on a separate floppy. Specifically, it stores a copy of the boot record, partition table, and CMOS information. Your system's internal hardware configuration, number and kind of drives installed, kind of graphics installed, amount of memory, and so forth, are stored in a CMOS (Complementary Metal Oxide Semiconductor, a special kind of chip). This information is retained even when your computer's power is off, as it is backed up by a battery. Only 286, 386, and 486 machines store setup information in a CMOS; XTs do not. If you lose any of this information, it can be restored to your machine from the rescue disk. (See " To Restore Rescue Disk.")

To Make a Disk Bootable

1. Start Disk Tools.

2. Highlight Make a Disk Bootable on the Procedures list.

3. Select Proceed.

4. Select the drive you want to make bootable. (If you select a floppy drive, insert the disk to be made bootable in the drive indicated and select OK.)

5. Select OK when the operation is complete to return to the Disk Tools main screen.

If you have ever tried to make a bootable floppy disk by using the SYS command in DOS, you have probably encountered the following problem: DOS reports that there is not enough room for the system even though the disk contains only a few small files. The problem is that the DOS system files must sit in a particular place at the beginning of the disk—cluster 2 and the following clusters. The first file copied to a disk not formatted with the system files, however, sits in cluster 2, so SYS reports insufficient room *because there is really a file in the way*. The Make a Disk Bootable function relocates data files at the beginning of the disk and copies the system files to the area beginning at cluster 2.

Make a Disk Bootable also works with hard disks, though it is less likely that you will need to use it with them. When you make a hard disk bootable, the function always reads the DOS system files from a floppy, so it is possible to replace the system files already on your hard disk with system files from a different version of DOS.

To Quit Disk Tools

• Select Quit in the Disk Tools dialog box, or press Esc.

To Recover from DOS's Recover

1. Start Disk Tools.

2. Highlight Recover from DOS's Recover on the Procedures list.

3. Select Proceed.

4. Select OK when you are finished reading the information screen.

5. Select the drive you want to fix. (Insert the damaged floppy in the indicated drive and select OK.)

6. Select OK after you read the warning screen.

7. Select Yes if you are absolutely sure you want to continue.

8. When the operation is complete, select OK to return to the Disk Tools main screen.

The RECOVER program in DOS is intended to recover data on disks whose directory structure has been corrupted. It ends up doing more harm than good, though, because it eliminates all sub-directories and renames all files, numbering them sequentially beginning with 0.

Recover from DOS's Recover has two uses:

- Use it *after* you have run DOS's RECOVER to return your disk to its pre-RECOVER condition (or at least a good approximation thereof).

- Use it *instead* of DOS's RECOVER to repair a disk with a damaged directory structure.

To Restore the Rescue Disk

1. Start Disk Tools.

2. Highlight Restore Rescue Diskette on the Procedures list.

3. Select Proceed.

4. Select Yes when you are absolutely sure you want to proceed.

5. Select the kind of information you want to restore (boot record, partition table, CMOS), and select OK.

6. Select the drive from which to restore information.

7. Insert the rescue disk in the indicated drive.

8. When the operation is complete, select OK to return to the Disk Tools main screen.

If you lose all or part of your boot record or partition table because of disk failure, you can restore this critical information and perhaps prevent the loss of most or all of your data.

If your CMOS information is lost (probably due to the death of the battery supplying power to the CMOS), you can restore this information instead of running your Setup program.

To Revive a Defective Disk

1. Start Disk Tools.

2. Highlight Revive a Defective Diskette on the Procedures list.

3. Select Proceed.

4. Select the drive you want to revive.

5. Insert the damaged disk in the indicated drive and select OK.

6. When the operation is complete, select OK to return to the Disk Tools main screen.

The Revive a Defective Diskette function can repair the bad clusters or sectors that may appear on your disks after they have been in use for a while. It reformats your disks *but without destroying any data*. Use this function if you get data read errors on a floppy that had been in good working order. You may also want to use the Norton Disk Doctor's Surface Test. (See "Norton Disk Doctor" in Part Four.)

To Start Disk Tools

- Select File ➤ Run. In the DOS Command text box, type in **disktool** and select OK; or

- Type **disktool** at the DOS prompt.

● SYNTAX

DISKTOOL [*/options*]

The options are:

/DOSRECOVER runs the Recover from DOS's RECOVER function.

/MAKEBOOT runs the Make a Disk Bootable function.

/RESTORE runs the Restore Rescue Diskette function.

/REVIVE runs the Revive a Defective Diskette function.

/SAVERESCUE runs the Create Rescue Diskette function.

IMAGE

The Image program protects your disks against accidental formatting. It saves essential disk information—the boot record, FAT, and root directory—to the file Image.DAT. This file can then be used by UnFormat to restore data to a formatted disk. (See "UnFormat," below.)

Unless you choose not to, Image is placed into your AUTOEXEC.BAT file when Norton Desktop for DOS is installed. It runs automatically every time you start your computer. You can run Image manually if you have made significant changes to your disk and want to have the most up-to-date information saved.

To Run Image

- Select File ➤ Run. In the DOS Command text box, type in **Image** [*drive:*] and click on OK; or

- Type in **Image** [*drive:*] at the DOS prompt.

● SYNTAX

Image [*drive:*] [/NOBACKUP]

drive: specifies the drive for which Image saves essential information. If *drive:* is omitted, the default drive is used.

/NOBACKUP causes Image not to create the backup file Image.BAK when it saves essential disk information.

● **NOTES**   Image can protect both floppy disks and hard disks from accidental formats. However, only floppies formatted with Norton's Safe Format can be recovered. Floppies formatted with a DOS format cannot be recovered, as they are completely overwritten in the process. (That is, the Image.DAT file, used to reconstruct the disk, is itself overwritten.) Hard disks, by contrast, can almost always be unformatted regardless of the formatting method. Hard-disk data is not overwritten during a DOS, or high-level, format.

The file Image.DAT *must* reside in the root directory in order for a disk to be properly unformatted. Image automatically places Image.DAT properly. Do not move this file.

NORTON CACHE

The Norton Cache is a fast, flexible disk cache. Using it can substantially increase the effective speed of your computer, if you have the memory to support its use. You should have a minimum of 384K of free extended or expanded memory available before opting to use Norton Cache.

CONFIGURING NORTON CACHE

Norton Cache has many options for changing its configuration to suit your needs and the variations in different systems. However, if you are not an experienced and knowledgeable user, we recommend that you stick to the default configuration, with one important difference. That difference is to turn off any delay in writing changed information to disk. This will make Norton Cache somewhat slower in certain situations, but greatly reduces the risk of data loss. The loss in speed is worth the increased comfort level.

To Configure Norton Cache

1.   Choose File ➤ Run or press Ctrl+O to turn on the DOS command line.

2.   Key in **ndconfig** and press Enter to start the Norton Configuration program.

3.   Select Startup Programs.

4.   Highlight Start Norton Cache and press the spacebar, or
click on Configure

5.   Choose from the options offered and then select OK when
you have finished, or Cancel to abort any changes.

6.   Select Edit to view the changes Norton Desktop will make
to your configuration files, or select Save to accept them.

7.   Select Quit to exit the configuration program, and then
select Exit to DOS to return to Norton Desktop.

8.   Finally, exit Norton Desktop for DOS and reboot your computer to allow the changes to take effect.

● OPTIONS: REGULAR

Loading   Controls from where Norton Desktop is loaded.

- **Do Not Load the Norton Cache** turns off the loading of
Norton Cache.

- **Load from CONFIG.SYS** loads the Norton Cache as
a device driver in your CONFIG.SYS file. This prevents
the cache from being unloaded from the DOS prompt,
but makes it compatible with a broader range of
hardware and software.

- **Load from AUTOEXEC.BAT** loads the Norton Cache
from your AUTOEXEC.BAT file.

High Memory   Controls where the cache program itself is
loaded.

- **Load in High Memory** will load the cache program
into high memory if there is enough available. This
option requires a 386 or 486 computer and a memory
manager such as EMM386.EXE or QEMM386. If you're
not sure how much high memory is available, choose
this option anyway. If there is insufficient high memory,
it will load Norton Cache into low memory.

- **Load in Low Memory** loads the cache program into low memory.

Cache Options   Controls the caching of floppy drives and whether the cache does its writes in the background.

- **Cache Floppy Drives A: and B:** will turn on the caching of floppy drives. This is not recommended, *especially* if IntelliWrites is turned on.

- **Enable IntelliWrites** turns on background processing of write requests. While this can make Norton Cache substantially faster, it can lead to data loss in the event of a power failure or other problem. The default value is on, but we recommend you turn this off by clearing the check box.

Memory Usage   Controls the type and amount of memory Norton Cache uses for its data buffers.

- **Expanded** uses expanded memory for the cache buffers. This option requires LIM4-compatible EMS. Use this option only if you have an IBM-XT compatible computer or have no available extended memory.

- **Extended** uses extended memory for the cache buffers. This is the preferred option and must be used for any computer that will be using Microsoft Windows.

- **Conventional** will use conventional DOS memory for the cache buffers. We recommend against this option.

- **DOS** sets the maximum amount of memory used by the cache when running DOS programs.

- **Windows** sets the maximum amount of memory used by the cache when running Microsoft Windows.

● OPTIONS: ADVANCED

Buffering   Controls the size and behavior of the cache buffers.

- **Size of the Read-ahead Buffer** controls how much of the disk Norton Cache reads ahead at a time. The default is 8 KB, but acceptable values are 0 to 64 KB.

Increasing this value can improve performance unless
the files are fragmented.

- **Size of the Write-back Buffer** controls the amount of
  data that Norton Cache writes to the disk at a time
  when using IntelliWrites. A value of 0 disables Intelli-
  Writes. For maximum performance, this value should
  be set to the size of a single track of your hard disk.

- **Size of the Cache Buffer Blocks** controls the size of the
  blocks Norton Cache uses to cache contiguous sectors.
  Valid values are 512, 1024, 2048, 4096, and 8192 bytes.

- **Delay Before Sectors are Written** the maximum time,
  in seconds and hundredths of a second, that Norton
  will delay before writing changed data to the hard disk.
  The maximum value is 59-$99/100$ seconds. Higher values
  can increase the efficiency and performance of the
  cache but greatly increase the risk of data loss. *We
  strongly recommend that you set this to zero for maximum
  safety.*

- **Don't Wait for Write-back to Display DOS Prompt**
  causes Norton Cache to return the DOS prompt quickly,
  even while a disk write is being conducted in the background.

- **Wait for Disk Writes (Multi-Tasking Off)** should always be checked if running Windows, DESQview, or
  another multitasking environment.

Optimize   Lets you choose from one of three preconfigured
sets of options for buffering.

- **Speed** is the default choice if Advanced Options is not
  chosen. This option includes 1-second write delays.

- **Efficiency** also uses a 1-second write delay, but uses
  smaller write-back and cache block buffers.

- **Memory** uses the absolute minimum values to reduce
  the amount of memory used by the cache itself. This option includes no read-ahead or write-back buffers, and
  no write delay.

USING NORTON CACHE

Once you have Norton Cache configured, there are a number of command line switches that let you see and control the behavior of the cache.

To Load Norton Cache

1. Choose Configure ➤ Startup Programs.

2. Select Start Norton Cache.

3. Select Save to write changes to your configuration files without editing them, Edit to view and modify any changes made, or Configure to change the default settings for Norton Cache first.

4. Exit Norton Desktop and reboot your computer for the changes to take effect.

To Use the Command Line Options

There are numerous command line options that let you see and control the cache parameters.

1. Select File ➤ Run.

2. Key in **ncache2 /OPTION**, where OPTION is one or more of the following:

- **–A** deactivates Norton Cache. This is recommended before using a non-Norton program that will write directly to the hard disk, such as a disk defragmentation program.

- **A** reactivates Norton Cache.

- **DELAY=ss.hh** sets the current maximum write delay in seconds and hundredths of a second.

- **DUMP** causes Norton Cache to write the current buffers to disk, regardless of the write delay setting.

- **MULTI=ON | OFF** turns on or off the multitasking features of Norton Cache.

- **QUICK=ON | OFF** turns on or off the quick return of the DOS prompt on disk writes.

- **QUIET** turns on quiet mode. Only errors will be reported.

- **REPORT** displays a detailed report of the current status and parameters of Norton Cache.

- **RESET** writes any pending writes to disk, and clears all of the cache buffers.

- **SAVE** saves the current configuration of Norton Cache as the default by writing to NCACHE.INI.

- **STATUS** displays the current status of Norton Cache.

- **UNINSTALL** will uninstall Norton Cache if Norton Cache was not loaded from the CONFIG.SYS and was the last TSR loaded.

- **INSTALL** reloads Norton Cache after it has been uninstalled.

SMARTCAN

SmartCan provides an invaluable additional layer of protection for your files. If you have SmartCan loaded and enabled, you can use UnErase to recover any deleted file.

To Configure SmartCan

1. Type **smartcan** at the DOS prompt.

2. The Configure SmartCan dialog box opens, as shown in Figure 5.1.

3. The Enable SmartCan checkbox will be marked; Unchecking this box will disable SmartCan. Deleted files will not be automatically saved and already-preserved files will not be purged.

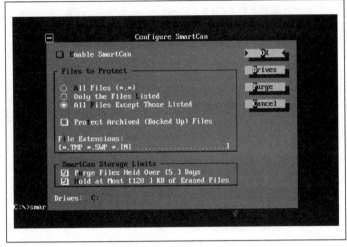

Figure 5.1: The Configure SmartCan dialog box

4. Select the files to protect.

- **All Files** will protect every deleted file.
- **Only the Files Listed** will protect only the files whose extensions are included on the File Extensions line.
- **All Files Except Those Listed** will protect all files except those whose extensions are included on the File Extensions line. This is the default, with the file extensions .TMP, .SWP and .INI specified as being unprotected. However, your system may differ, particularly if you have Norton Desktop for Windows installed.
- **Protect Archived (Backed Up) Files** will protect files that have not changed since they were backed up. The default is off, because it is assumed that accidentally deleted files of this type could be retrieved from a backup.

5. Select SmartCan Storage Limits. The default is to purge files held more than 5 days and to hold at most 2048 KB (2 MB) of files. Again, your system may show different default settings. If you have installed Norton Desktop for Windows elsewhere on your system, SmartCan will pick up the settings you have chosen for that program's Smart-Erase.

6. Select the drives to protect by clicking on the Drives button. Select individual drives from the list on the left of the Drives box or make an inclusive selection from the Drive Types box. Click on OK when finished.

7. When you have finished configuring SmartCan, select OK to save your settings.

To Enable SmartCan

• If you did not choose to install SmartCan at the time of your original installation, you will need to run the install program again. See Part One for information.

• If you installed SmartCan but did not enable it, select Configure ➤ Startup Programs. Double-click on Start SmartCan or press the spacebar to add a check mark. Click on the Save button. This adds SmartCan to your AUTOEXEC.BAT file.

● **NOTE**   After installing SmartCan into your Startup Programs, exit Norton Desktop for DOS and reboot your computer. This automatically enables it.

To Purge Files Manually

SmartCan automatically deletes protected files after the specified time or when the allotted space is exceeded. However, you can easily purge files manually.

1. Type **smartcan** at the DOS prompt.

2. In the Configure SmartCan dialog box, select the Purge button.

3. Select Drive to select the drive from which to purge.

4. Use the spacebar or the mouse to select the files to be purged. You can also click on the Tag button and enter a wildcard file specification.

5. When you have finished your selection, select the Purge button.

6. Click on the Cancel button to leave the Purge Deleted Files box, or select another drive to purge.

To Turn SmartCan On and Off

If you are doing some major housecleaning on your disk and want to turn SmartCan off temporarily, you can do so without opening the Configure SmartCan dialog box.

At the DOS prompt type **smartcan /off**. To turn it back on, go to the DOS prompt and type **smartcan /on**.

If you have forgotten whether SmartCan is on or off, go to the DOS prompt and type **smartcan /status**, and a message will inform you whether SmartCan is enabled or disabled.

● **NOTE** If you turn SmartCan off, you may get a message that Smartcan cannot be removed because of conflict with other TSRs. Nevertheless, the program *is* disabled and will not protect files until turned back on.

UNFORMAT

UnFormat can recover data from a hard disk that has been formatted or damaged by a virus or power failure. UnFormat can also recover a diskette that has been formatted with Safe Format.

To Unformat a Hard Disk

1. Insert a bootable diskette in drive A, with the same DOS version used to format your hard disk. Reboot your system.

2. Remove the DOS diskette, insert disk 2 (the Emergency–Data Recovery disk) from your Norton Desktop for DOS installation disks in drive A, and key in **unformat**.

3. Read the message in the UnFormat dialog box and click on Continue.

4. Select the drive you wish to unformat and click on OK.

5. You will be asked if IMAGE or MIRROR (from DOS 5.x) was previously used to save information on the drive to be unformatted. Select Yes or No, as appropriate.

6. Select Yes in the confirmation box.

7. If you answered Yes in step 5, and the information has been saved, the IMAGE or MIRROR information will display. Click on OK. Select Yes in the Absolutely Sure box. Then select Full in the Full or Partial Restore box.

If you answered Yes in step 5 and the IMAGE or MIRROR information is not available, select Yes to proceed with the unformat without IMAGE or MIRROR information.

If you answered No in step 5, go to step 8.

8. Click on OK, once or twice, until the unformat is complete.

● **NOTE** You can select a partial restoration in step 7. Toggle on Boot Record, File Allocation Table, or Root Directory to select these areas to be restored.

To unformat a floppy disk, type **unformat** from the DOS prompt; or select File ➤ Run, type **unformat** in the DOS Command text box, and select OK. Follow steps 3 through 8 under "To UnFormat a Hard Disk."

Appendix A

Batch Enhancer

BATCH ENHANCER

Batch Enhancer allows you to greatly increase the convenience and flexibility of DOS batch files. There are 17 Batch Enhancer commands, each with parameters and options to perform specific functions.

● SYNTAX

BE *command*

command is one of seventeen possible BE commands, each having its own options and switches. Descriptions of these commands follow.

ASK

Puts custom menus or prompts in batch files.

● SYNTAX

BE ASK "*prompt*", [*keys*] [**default**=*key*] [**timeout**=*secs*] [**adjust**=*#*] [*color*] [*/debug*]

"*prompt* " is the text of the menu or prompt to be displayed (must be enclosed in quotation marks).

keys are the keys that are valid responses to *prompt*. Pressing a key other than one listed causes a warning beep to sound. ASK provides conditional branching by returning a different DOS ERRORLEVEL code for each key in *keys*. The first key returns ERRORLEVEL 1, the second ERRORLEVEL 2, and so on.

default=*key* specifies the default choice.

timeout=*secs* specifies the number of seconds ASK waits before automatically assuming the default. If no timeout is specified, ASK will wait forever.

adjust=# adds a specified number (integer) to the DOS ERROR-LEVEL code returned by each key in *keys*. ASK provides conditional branching by returning a different DOS ERRORLEVEL code for each key in *keys*. The first key returns ERRORLEVEL 1, the second ERRORLEVEL 2, and so on. If, then, one of the menu choices calls up another menu, its first key will also return ERRORLEVEL 1 and its second key ERRORLEVEL 2. To prevent a conflict, use adjust=# to change the value of the ERRORLEVEL codes returned by one of the two menus. The maximum value for # is 254.

color specifies the color of the prompt. Valid colors are black, blue, green, cyan, red, magenta, yellow, and white.

/debug displays the exit code returned (ERRORLEVEL) as modified by the adjust= parameter.

BEEP

Plays tones for a specified duration and of a specified pitch. Tones can be specified on the command line or grouped together in a file.

● SYNTAX

BE BEEP [/D#] [/F#] [/R#] [/W#]

Or

BE BEEP *filename* [/E]

/D# specifies the duration of a tone in eighteenths of a second; # must be positive.

/F# specifies the frequency of a tone in hertz; # must be positive.

/R# specifies the number of times a tone is repeated; # must be positive.

/W# specifies the interval between tones in eighteenths of a second; # must be positive.

filename specifies the name of a file containing tones to be played. Tones are specified in *filename* just as they are on the command line by using the switches listed above.

/E echoes comments in *filename* to the screen. Comments are set off from commands by a semicolon. To be echoed, they must be enclosed in quotation marks (for example, /F523; "Middle C").

BOX

Draws a box at specified screen coordinates.

● SYNTAX

BE BOX *TLrow TLcol BRrow BRcol* **[Single|Double]** [*color*]

TLrow TLcol are the screen coordinates of the top-left corner of the box. *TLrow* is the row in which this corner sits, and *TLcol* is the column.

BRrow BRcol are the screen coordinates of the bottom-right corner of the box. *BRrow* is the row in which this corner sits, and *BRcol* is the column.

Single | Double specifies whether the box is drawn with single or double lines.

color specifies the color of the box. Valid colors are the same as for the ASK prompt.

CLS

Clears the screen.

● SYNTAX

BE CLS [*color*]

color is an optional parameter to set the screen color after clearing. Valid colors are the same as for the ASK prompt.

DELAY

Pauses batch-file execution for a specified length of time.

● **SYNTAX**

BE DELAY #

specifies the duration of the pause in eighteenths of a second;
must be positive.

EXIT

Ends the execution of a script file before the end of the file is
reached.

● **SYNTAX**

BE EXIT

GOTO

Allows for selective execution of BE commands within *datafile*. BE
essentially supports the DOS GOTO batch file command, but
within BE *datafiles*. See your DOS manual for more details.

● **SYNTAX**

BE *datafile* **[[GOTO]***label***]**

datafile is the file containing BE commands.

label is the name of the label within *datafile* marking the group
of commands you want to execute. Labels in *datafile* are func-
tionally identical to labels in DOS batch files.

JUMP

Branches to a label in a script file based on the ERRORLEVEL (exit
code) of the previous command.

● **SYNTAX**

BE JUMP name*1* **[, name***2* **[,...name***n***]] [/default:***name***]**

name is a valid label that appears in the script file.

/default:*name* is the label to branch to if the exit code is zero or the exit code is greater than the number of names supplied.

MONTHDAY

Returns the day of the month to the batch file as an exit code.

● SYNTAX

BE MONTHDAY [/debug]

/debug displays the exit code returned (ERRORLEVEL).

PRINTCHAR

Writes a character to the screen a specified number of times.

● SYNTAX

BE PRINTCHAR *char*, # [*color*]

char is the character to be written.

specifies the number of times the character is to be written.

color specifies the color of the character. Valid colors are the same as for the ASK prompt.

REBOOT

Performs either a warm or cold boot of the computer.

● SYNTAX

BE REBOOT [/verify] [/c]

/verify asks for a Y/N response to confirm the reboot.

/c performs a cold boot.

ROWCOL

Positions the cursor and optionally writes text at specified screen coordinates.

● SYNTAX

BE ROWCOL *row col* [*text*] [*color*]

row is the row in which the cursor is positioned.

col is the column in which the cursor is positioned.

text is the text to be written at the new cursor position. If text includes a space, the whole parameter must be enclosed in quotes.

color specifies the color of the text. Valid colors are the same as for the ASK prompt.

SA

The Screen Attributes command. Sets text, background, and border colors. For SA to be used, the ANSI.SYS driver must be loaded in your CONFIG.SYS file.

● SYNTAX

BE SA Normal|Underline|Reverse [/N]

Or

BE SA [*intensity*] [*textcolor*] [ON *background*] [/N] [/CLS]

Normal resets all attributes, including *underline* or *reverse*.

Underline causes the text to be underlined.

Reverse switches the foreground and background colors.

intensity specifies the intensity of the foreground text. Can be set to Bright or Blinking.

textcolor specifies the color of the foreground text. Valid colors are black, blue, green, cyan, red, magenta, yellow, and white.

background specifies the background color. Valid colors are the same as for *textcolor*.

/N leaves the border color unchanged. (Normally, the border color is automatically set to the background color.) Use this switch to change the background color but not the border color.

/CLS clears the screen after colors are changed.

SHIFTSTATE

Reports the status of the Shift, Ctrl, and Alt keys.

● SYNTAX

BE SHIFTSTATE [/debug]

/debug displays the ERRORLEVEL (exit code) returned. The exit codes are:

1   Right Shift key
2   Left Shift key
4   Ctrl key
8   Alt key

TRIGGER

Stops the execution of a batch file until a specified time.

● SYNTAX

BE TRIGGER *hours:minutes* **[AM|PM]**

hours:minutes is the time in 24-hour format.

AM or PM will allow specifying time in 12-hour format.

WEEKDAY

Returns the day of the week to the batch file as an exit code (ER-RORLEVEL).

● **SYNTAX**

BE WEEKDAY [/debug]

/debug displays the exit code (ERRORLEVEL) returned. Sunday is returned as 1, Monday as 2, and so on.

WINDOW

Draws a window at specified screen coordinates.

● **SYNTAX**

BE WINDOW *TLrow TLcol BRrow BRcol* [*color*] [**Explode**] [**Shadow**]

TLrow TLcol are the screen coordinates (row and column) of the top-left corner of the window.

BRrow BRcol are the screen coordinates (row and column) of the bottom-right corner of the window.

color specifies the color of the window. Valid colors are the same as for the ASK prompt.

Explode causes the window to expand from its center to its final position when it is drawn.

Shadow gives the window a three-dimensional look by drawing a shadow along the right and bottom edges of the window. The shadow does not obscure text underneath it.

Appendix B

Running in Norton Commander Mode

If you are a user of Norton Commander 3.0, you can make the Norton Desktop for DOS assume the same look. Many of the functions are the same, but there are some differences, as explained below. The explanations cover only those instances in which the menus are not the same as in Norton Commander 3.0. For information on how to use commands specific to Norton Commander 3.0, please see that program's documentation.

To Switch to Norton Commander Mode

1.   Select Configure ➤ Preferences.

2.   In the Desktop group, click on the Style prompt button.

3.   Select Norton Commander. Click on OK. The screen display changes to look like Norton Commander.

To Switch Back to Norton Desktop Display

1.   Select Options ➤ Configuration.

2.   In the Desktop group, click on the Norton Desktop radio button. Click on OK. The screen display changes back to the Norton Desktop.

Changes in the Norton Commander Panels

Though the panels look very much the same as those in Norton Commander 3.0, there are several new features.

- In the bottom right corner of each panel are upward- and downward-pointing arrows. Click on either to resize the panel vertically.

- On the right side of each panel is a scroll bar to scroll through the file listings.

- In the upper-left corner of each panel is a control box. Open the control box menu by pressing Alt+- (hyphen).

NORTON COMMANDER MODE MENUS

In this section, we describe only the menu commands that are *not* in Norton Commander 3.0.

Left/Right Menus

Entire Drive   A new command that shows every file on the selected drive, in order by file name. The directory for each file is shown in a second column.

Compressed File   Highlight a compressed file and then select this command to see the contents listing of an achive (compressed) file. Or you can select this command and type in the name of the file, use the prompt button to choose from a list of recent choices, or select Browse.

Files

Find File   Opens the Find File function of the Norton Desktop for DOS. See Part Three for information on Find.

Print   Prints the highlighted file.

Compress   Opens the Compress dialog box. See Part Two for details on Compress.

Commands

Copy Diskette, **Format Diskette**, and **Make Disk Bootable** See Part Four for information on diskette functions.

Menu Edit   Opens Norton Menu. See Part Four for details on using Norton Menu.

Associate   Opens the Associate file dialog box. See Part Three for information on associating files.

Options

Configuration   This opens the Configure Desktop dialog box, where you can choose between the Norton Desktop and Norton Commander screen displays. The other options in this window are identical to options in the Norton Commander Options ➤ Configuration menu. If you choose the Advanced button, the choices are the same as those in the Norton Desktop menu: Configure ➤ Preferences ➤ Advanced. See Part Two for information on these choices.

Startup Programs   See Part Two.

Video/Mouse   See "Screen" and "Mouse" in Part Two.

Screen Saver   See Part Two.

Printer   See Part Two.

Compression   See Part Three.

Editor   See Part Three.

Configure Link   See "Desktop Link" in Part Two.

Confirmation   See Part Two.

Utilities

Advise   See Part Five.

Calculator   See Part Four.

Calendar   See Part Four.

Network Message   See Part Four.

UnErase   See Part Four.

Speed Disk   See Part Four.

Norton Disk Doctor   See Part Four.

Norton Backup   See Part Four.

Norton AntiVirus   See Part Four.

System Information   See Part Four.

Scheduler   See Part Four.

Index

* (asterisk) wildcard character, 61–62
? (question mark) wildcard character, 61–62
@ sign, and starting macros, 146
| (pipe character), 61–62
386MAX (Qualitas), 12
80286 computers, memory on, 11
80386 computers, memory management on, 11–12

A

acceleration, of mouse, 25
accidental formatting
  labels and, 90
  protection against, 187–188
active command button, arrowheads on, 38
Address Book
  automatically adding sender address to, 93
  MCI Mail, 97–99
  opening, 101
addresses
  permanently deleting, 99
  undeleting, 99
Addresses menu, Auto-Add, 97
Advanced program level
  for backup, 128–131
  for compare, 140
  for restore, 143–144
Advise, 182
aliases, 104
Alt key, status of, 206

AntiVirus. *See* Norton Anti-Virus
AntiVirus Intercept, 116
Append To (File menu), 168
appending backups, 130
applications. *See* programs
Archive attribute, 52
  backups and, 125
  restore operation and, 144
arguments, prompt for, 108
ASCII characters, 31, 57, 176, 178
  search for, 171
ASK command (Batch Enhancer), 200–201
Associate (File menu), 50–52
associating file name extensions with programs, 50–52
asterisk (*) wildcard character, 61–62
attributes, 52–53
  displaying, 80
  and file searches, 62–63
Auto-Add (Addresses menu), 97
Auto Inoculate, 118
Auto Weekly test, by Norton Disk Doctor, 150
Autobuild (File menu), 106
AUTOEXEC.BAT file, 4, 6
  copying, 12
  editing, 13–14, 46
  Image in, 187
  NMENU in, 102
  Norton Backup and, 122
  Norton Cache in, 189
  SmartCan in, 195

viewing, 167
automating backups, 144–147
autosave menu files, 104

B

backedup files, comparing
    with hard disk files, 138–140
background
    color of, 40, 205
    on screen, 38
Backup To button, 127
Backup window, 124–131
backups. *See also* catalogs, back-
    up set
    appending, 130
    automating, 144–147
    to copy files, 125
    first time, 120–122
    overwrite warning before,
        130–131
    scheduling, 8
    selecting files for, 133–134
    types of, 125
Basic program level
    for backup, 126–128
    for Compare window, 138
    for restoring backups, 142–
        143
Batch Enhancer, 200–207
Batch Enhancer Plus, install-
    ing, 7
batch files
    creating from file list, 64–65
    in menus, 106, 109
    for Scheduler, 153–154
baud rate
    for Desktop Link, 22
    for Norton Mail, 93
beep
    during backup, 127, 129

during compare operation,
    139
after virus location, 118
BEEP command (Batch Enhan-
    cer), 201–202
boot process, 204
    loading Norton Cache
        during, 8
    loading Scheduler/Screen
        Saver during, 8
boot record
    restoring, 186
    saving, 187
boot sector, repairing, 114
boot sector viruses, on floppy
    drives, 119
bootable disks, 12, 183–184
    creating, 91
    formatting, 90
    for rescue disk, 5
border, color of, 205
BOX command (Batch Enhan-
    cer), 202
Browse Extension (Add Menu
    Item dialog box), 108
Browse for Print dialog box, 68
button bar
    backup options, 134–136
    configuring, 18–19
    Edit, 23
    updating, 30
buttons, changing commands
    for, 18

C

cables, to connect computers,
    86
cache buffers, 190–191
Calculator, 84
Calendar, 85

carbon copies, of MCI Mail, 101
case sensitivity
  for erased clusters, 176
  in text searches, 59, 61
catalogs, backup set, 138, 141
  for compare, 139
  printing, 143
  for restore, 142, 143
  retaining old backup, 127
  storing on tape, 128
Change Drive (File menu), 169
Checksum error checking, 22
chime, as backup prompt, 129
CHKDSK command (DOS), 9
Clear (Edit menu), 59
client, 86
Clock, configuring, 19
cloning files, for Desktop Link,
  22–23
Close (File menu), 57
CLS command (Batch Enhan-
  cer), 202
clusters, 155, 163
  in erased files, 178
  repairing, 186
  statistics on, 162
  for unerasing file, 175
CMOS information, 183, 186
CMOS Status screen, 166
CMOS tests, skipping, 148
color palette, 2
colors, 205
  customizing, 38–40
  for Norton Backup, 123
  on screen, 38
COM port, 93
command line, 71
  options for Norton Backup,
    146–147
  options for Norton Cache, 192

parameters, and associations,
  51–52
starting Norton Menu from,
  103
commands, changing button
  assignment, 18
communications port, for
  Desktop Link, 21
Compare window
  in Norton Backup, 138–140
  program levels for, 138–139
  selecting files, 139–140
Compare Windows (Window
  menu), 81
comparing directories in drive
  windows, 80–81
Compress (File menu), 19–20,
  53–54
compressed files
  from backup, 128–129
  viewing contents, 54
compressed printing, 31
compressing files, 19–20, 53–54
Compression (Configure
  menu), 19–20
CompuServe, virus definition
  files from, 115–116
computers
  booting, 204
  connecting, 86–87
  copying and moving files
    between, 21–23
  linking for file transfer, 85–87
  rebooting after defragmenta-
    tion, 163
conditional branching, 200
CONFIG.SYS file, 4, 6
  copying, 12
  editing, 13, 46
  Norton AntiVirus in, 119
  Norton Backup and, 122

Norton Cache in, 189
viewing, 167
Configure menu
Button Bar, 18–19
Clock, 19
Compression, 19–20
Confirmation, 21
Desktop Link, 21
Edit Pull-downs, 33, 35, 36
Editor, 24
Load Pull-downs, 32–33
Network, 26
Password, 26–27
Preferences, 27–30, 43, 210
Preferences ➤ Advanced, 77
Printer, 30
Save Configuration, 43
Screen Saver, 41
Startup Programs, 45, 192
Video/Mouse, 24, 37–40
configuring
Norton Backup, 122–124
Norton Cache, 188–191
Norton Desktop for DOS,
18–47
Norton Disk Doctor, 147–148
Norton Mail, 92
panes, 78
saving, 43
Confirmation (Configure
menu), 21
Connected Network Users box,
112
conventional memory, for
cache buffers, 190
Copy (Edit menu), 58
Copy (File menu), 55
Copy Diskette (Disk menu), 87
copy protection
backups and, 135

and unmovable files, 161
copying
backup process for, 125
Desktop Link, 21–23
diskettes, 87–88
files, 55
menu items, 109
text, 58
CPU Speed screen, 167
CRC error checking, 22
Create Batch (Options menu),
64
Create File (File menu), 176
Ctrl key, status of, 206
cursor
batch command to position,
205
as rectangle or underscore, 38
custom filter, for file display, 78
custom installation, 2
custom items, adding to pull-
down menus, 36
custom menus, 103–104
in batch files, 200–201
Cut (Edit menu), 58
cutting text, 58

D

.DAT file name extension, 171
data compression, in backup,
128–129
data format (printer option), 31
data fragments, search for
deleted, 171
data verification
in backup, 128
during restore, 144
database files
search erased disk for, 171
searching text in, 61

date
and backup file selection, 135
for compressed file, 20
displaying file creation, 79
sorting files by, 163, 173
day of week, batch command
for, 206
.DBF file name extension, 171
default settings
for editor, 24
resetting button bar to, 18
returning colors to, 40
defective disks, reviving, 186
DELAY command (Batch En-
hancer), 202–203
Delete (File menu), 55
deleted files, recovering, 2
deleting
addresses, 98
addresses permanently, 99
associations, 51
confirmation for, 104
disk labels, 90–91
files, 55–56
files after compressing, 53
infected files, 114–115
MCI Mail accounts, 95
menu items, 36–37, 110
menus, 105
in Norton Mail, 92
printer configuration file, 32
subdirectories, 55–56
text, 59
Deselect (File menu), 72
Desktop Editor, 56
Desktop Link, 86
copying, 21–23
DESQview, Norton Cache and,
191
device drivers, loading in high
memory, 13

Device Drivers screen, 167
dial type, for Norton Mail, 93
Differential backups, 125
appending, 131
command line option for, 146
directories
changing, 169
comparing in drive window,
80–81
copying or moving, 28
creating, 67
creating during restore, 142,
143
displaying, 80
listing files in current, 170
listing prior to backup, 128
for Norton Desktop, 3
for Norton Mail, 94
placement at beginning of
disk, 158
prune and graft for, 70
renaming, 71
repairing structure, 185
searches for files in erased,
172
selecting for backup, 133
sorting by, 173
specifying order in Speed
Disk, 159–160
temporary for compressing
files, 20
Directory (Scan menu), 114
disk cache. *See* Norton cache
Disk Characteristics screen, 166
disk information, viewing, 162
disk map, walking, 162–163
Disk menu
Copy Diskette, 87
Format Diskette, 88, 154
Label Disk, 90
Make Disk Bootable, 91

Prune & Graft, 70
Serve Remote Link, 86
disk optimization, 155
  scheduling, 8
disk problems, diagnosing, 182
disk size, 162
disk space, 162
  displaying free, 30
  unfragmenting, 158, 163
Disk Summary screen, 166
Disk Tools, 183–187
  installing, 7
  and Scheduler disabled, 154
DISKCOPY command (DOS),
  87
diskettes, 87–91
  backup transfers to, 131
  boot sector viruses on, 119
  caching, 190
  configuring for formatting, 89
  configuring for Norton Back-
    up, 123
  copying, 87–88
  error correction on, 127
  formatting, 88–90
  formatting system, 12
  Image protection of, 188
  labels for, 90
  prompt before overwriting,
    127
  proprietary format for back-
    up, 127
  scanning with Norton Anti-
    Virus, 28
  unformatting, 197
disks. *See also* diskettes; hard
  disks
  bootable, 12, 183–184
  placing files at beginning,
    156–157

reformatting without data
  destruction, 186
testing and repairing, 149–151
DMA Test, 124
document files, in file pane, 78
documents, searching text in,
  61
DOS 5, 10
  loading TSRs high with, 12–14
DOS background, command
  line, 71
DOS Background (View
  menu), 40, 66
DOS command line, launching
  file from, 66
DOS commands
  CHKDSK, 9
  DISKCOPY, 87
  LOADHIGH, 14
  RECOVER, 184–185
  SYS, 91, 184
DOS format, 89, 188
DOS system files, transferring
  during formatting, 90
double-clicking, speed for, 24
Draft Folder, 92
drag & drop, and subdirectories, 28
Drive (Scan menu), 113
drive icons, refreshing, 30
drive icons (Preferences), 29
drive selector, in drive window, 76
drive windows, 75–81
  comparing directories in,
    80–81
  moving, 77
  opening, 75
  parts of, 76–77
  refreshing, 30, 77
  selecting files in, 71–72

size adjustment, 77–78
drives
  changing, 169
  excluding from testing, 152
  listing all files on, 170
  Norton AntiVirus scan of, 113
  selecting for defragmenting, 157
  uninoculating, 117–119

E

EBCDIC data format, 31
Edit (button bar), 23
Edit (File menu), 23, 56
Edit menu
  Add, 106, 109
  Clear, 59, 110
  Copy, 58, 109
  Cut, 58, 110
  Menu Title, 103
  Modify, 110
  Paste, 58, 110
  Select All, 58
Edit Pull-downs (Configure menu), 33, 35, 36
editing
  files, 56–60
  menu items on pull-down menu, 36–37
Editing Startup Files screen, 4
Editor, configuring, 23–24
Emergency–Data Recovery disk, 2
EMM386.EXE memory manager, 11
EMS address type, 98
Enter Moves Focus (mouse option), 25
erased directories, search for files in, 172

erased disks, search for text on, 171–172
erased files, search for clusters, 175
error checking, by Desktop Link, 22
error correction
  during backup, 131
  on diskettes, 127
  by Norton Disk Doctor, 149
error messages
  in backup report, 130
  customizing from Norton Disk Doctor, 147–148
  interpreting, 182
executable files. *See* programs
EXIT command (Batch Enhancer), 203
Exit Menu after Execution (Add Menu dialog box), 108
expanded memory, for cache buffers, 190
Expanded Memory screen, 166
Expanded Memory Specification, 11
exploding windows, 207
Export (File menu), 105
extended memory, 11
  for cache buffers, 190
Extended Memory screen, 166

F

Fast Mouse Reset, 25
FAX address type, 98
Faxline, virus definition files from, 116
File (Scan menu), 114
file allocation table (FAT), 168
  saving, 187
  saving copy of, 8

file creation date, displaying, 79
File Details (View menu), 79
File fragmentation report, 161
file lists
  in backup report, 130
  creating batch files from,
    64–65
  of current directory, 170
  including existing files on, 169
  sorting, 172–173
  viewing file contents, 178
File menu
  Append To, 168
  Associate, 50–52
  Autobuild, 106
  Change Directory, 169
  Change Drive, 169
  Close, 57
  Compress, 19–20, 53–54
  Copy, 55
  Create File, 176
  Delete, 55, 105
  Deselect, 72
  Edit, 23, 56
  Export, 105
  Find, 60–65
  Insert, 58
  Make Directory, 67
  Manual UnErase, 175
  Move, 67–68
  New, 56, 104–105
  Open, 56, 68, 103
  Open Setup, 132
  Print, 58, 68–69
  Print Setup, 58
  Properties, 52, 69
  Rename, 71, 170
  Run, 66
  Save, 57
  Save As, 57
  Save Setup As, 132

Select, 72
Select Group, 174
UnErase To, 177
Unselect, 178
Unselect Group, 177
View, 74
View All Directories, 170
View Current Directory, 170
file name extensions
  associating with programs,
    50–52
  .DAT, 171
  .DBF, 171
  .NAB, 105–106
  .NDM, 33, 37
  .NMF, 105
  .NPS, 31
  for Quattro Pro, 51
  .RPT, 127, 130
  .SET, 133
  sorting by, 172
  sorting files by, 164
  .TXT, 171
  .WK1, 171
  .ZIP, 53
file names
  for erased files, 174
  sorting files by, 164
  for unerased files, 176–177
file pane, 78
  changing details in, 79–80
  launching file from, 66
  in Select Backup Files win-
    dow, 133
  sort order in, 80
  Speed Search box for, 77
File Server combination box,
  112
file size
  for backup, 131
  displaying, 79

sorting files by, 164, 173

file transfer, linking computers for, 85

files. *See also* attributes
adding data to, 168
backup to single, 128
closing, 57
comparing, 126
comparing backup with hard disk, 138–140
compressing, 19–20, 53–54
copying, 55
deleting, 55–56
displaying creation date, 79
editing, 56–60
filters for display of, 78–79
fragmented, 155
inserting one in another, 57–58
launching, 65–66
moving, 67–68
overwriting during restore, 144
printing, 58, 68–69
properties of, 69–70
protecting with SmartCan, 194
reinoculating, 115
renaming, 71, 170
repairing infected, 117
saving, 57
scanning for viruses, 114
selecting in drive windows, 71–72
sending report to, 165
sort order for, 160
specifying placement during optimization, 156
statistics on, 162
tagging for unerasure, 173

uncompressing, 54
unerasing to new location, 177
unmovable in Speed Disk, 160–161
untagging, 177–178
viewing, 72–75
viewing information about, 178

Filter (View menu), 78–79
filters, for file display, 78–79
Find (File menu), 60–65
Find (Search menu), 59
floppy-disk compatibility tests, 121–122
floppy disks. *See* diskettes
folder, for MCI messages, 92
Format Diskette (Disk menu), 88, 154
formatting
during backup, 127
diskettes, 88–90
hard disks, 89
protection against accidental, 187–188
system diskettes, 12
tapes during backup, 128
fragmented files, 155
free disk space
displaying, 30
unfragmenting, 158, 163
Full backup, 125
command line option for, 146
overwriting when, 131
Full copy backup, command line option for, 146
Full Install, 2
Full Page Read option, for Norton Mail, 92

G

Go To button (Advise), 182
Go to command, when viewing files, 73
GOTO command (Batch Enhancer), 203
grafting directories, 70
graphic files, viewing, 74–75
graphical display, for Norton Backup, 123
graphical mouse, 25
Graphics
  installing, 6
  manipulating, 75
group of files
  tagging for unerase, 174
  untagging, 177

H

Hard Disk Speed screen, 167
hard disks
  accidental formatting, 2
  bootable, 184
  data recovery from damaged, 196
  formatting, 89
  Image protection of, 188, 197
  installing program on, 2
  unformatting, 196–197
Hardware Interrupts screen, 166
headers, 31
Help menu, Advise, 182
hex characters, viewing, 176, 178
hidden files, 52
  backups and, 135
  in file pane, 79
high DOS memory, 10–11

high memory
  for cache program, 189
  loading memory-resident programs in, 10–12
High Memory Area, 11
HIMEM.SYS file, 11
hotkeys
  assigning, 109
  for menu items, 104, 107
  for screen saver, 42

I

IBM PC/AT computers, memory on, 11
icons, 104
  displaying, 79
Image.DAT file, 187, 188
Image Information, saving during formatting, 90
Image program, 187–188
  installing, 7
  running at shutdown, 45
  and Scheduler disabled, 154
  as startup program, 8, 46
  UnErase and, 179
  UnFormat and, 197
imploding files, for compression, 20
Import (Setup menu), 96
importing mail, to Norton Mail, 96
In Folder, 100
Include/Exclude List dialog box, 134, 135
Include Files dialog box, 134, 135
Incremental backups, 125
  appending, 131
  command line option for, 146
infected files, 114–115, 117

Information menu
  Disk Statistics, 162
  Map Legend, 162
  Walk Map, 162–163
information screen
  printing, 165
  viewing, 166–167
Insert (File menu), 58
insert key (Preferences), 28
inserting, one file in another,
    57–58
Install Program Files screen, 3
installing, 2, 7
  Norton Desktop for DOS, 2–9
  Norton Menu as shell, 102
  tools, 6–7
IntelliWrites, 190

J

JUMP command (Batch En-
    hancer), 203–204

K

keystroke options (Prefer-
    ences), 28–29

L

Label Disk (Disk menu), 90
labels, for diskettes, 90
landscape orientation, 32
launching files, 65–66
left-handed mouse, 25
lines
  number displayed, 38
  spacing, 31
  wrapping, 31
lines per screen, for Norton
    Backup, 123
Link PCs, 85–87

Load Pull-downs (Configure
    menu), 32–33
LOADHIGH command (DOS),
    14
log, of virus reports, 118
login name, for MCI Mail, 94
Lotus Express, importing from,
    96
Lotus spreadsheet files, in file
    pane, 79
low memory, cache program
    in, 190

M

macros, in Norton Backup,
    145–147
mail. *See* MCI Mail; Norton
    Mail
Mail menu
  Reply, 100
  Send/Receive, 100, 102
Make Directory (File menu), 67
Manual UnErase (File menu),
    175
map legend, viewing, 162
margins, on printed copy, 31
master environment area, 30
Match Upper/Lowercase (Op-
    tions menu), 61
MCI Accounts (Setup menu), 94
MCI Instant address type, 98
MCI Mail
  Address Book, 97–99
  carbon copies of, 101
  collecting, 100
  interface with, 91–102
  shutdown and, 45
  writing message for, 101–102
MCI Mail accounts, 92, 94–96
MCI messages, folder for, 92

MCI Telephone, setup for, 93
memory, 4
  for Norton Cache buffers, 190
  for Norton Desktop, 9–15
  scanning for viruses, 113
  for startup programs, 46
Memory Block List screen, 167
memory-resident programs, 10
  loading high with DOS 5,
    12–14
Memory Usage Summary
    screen, 166
Menu (Tools menu), 102
menu bar, adding pull-down
    menus to, 33–35
menu items
  copying, 109
  deleting, 110
  hotkeys for, 104
  modifying, 110
  in Norton Menu, 106–111
  password for, 110–111
Menu Title (Edit menu), 103
menus, 103–106
  changing titles, 103
  creating in Norton Menu,
    104–105
  creating for programs, 5, 9
  customizing, 103–104
  deleting, 105
  distributing to other users,
    105–106
  installing, 6
  password protection of, 26–27
  saving, 34–35
  updating automatically, 106
messages. *See also* error mes-
    sages
  description for mail, 92
  displaying at preset times, 152

including original in mail
    reply, 92–93
  from network, 26
  for Screen Saver, 42
  for virus detection, 119
  writing for MCI Mail, 101–102
Minimal install, 2
Mirror
  UnErase and, 179
  UnFormat and, 197
modem
  setup for Norton Mail, 93
  setup string for, 94
MONTHDAY command
    (Batch Enhancer), 204
More >> button, for Find, 62–63
mouse
  configuring, 24–25
  options for Norton Backup,
    123
  and screen saver, 42
mouse cursor, appearance of,
    25
Move (File menu), 67–68
moving
  drive windows, 77
  files, 67–68
  files between computers,
    21–23
multitasking environment,
    Norton Cache and, 191

N

.NAB file name extension, 105–
    106
navigation keys, 28–29
NDDUNDO.DAT file, 151
.NDM file name extension, 33,
    37
NetBIOS, 86

network drives, scanning for
  viruses, 118
network files
  comparing, 139
  restoring, 142
  retrying backup for, 126
Network Information screen,
  166
Network Message, 111–112
Network Performance Speed
  screen, 167
networks, 86
  backups on, 129–130
  configuring Desktop for,
  25–26
  disconnecting at shutdown, 45
  storing inoculation data for
  drives, 118
New (File menu), 56
.NMF file name extension, 105
Normal Text, on erased disk,
  171
Norton AntiVirus, 3, 112–120
  in CONFIG.SYS file, 119
  installing, 6
  running at shutdown, 45
  scanning floppy disk with, 28
  as startup program, 46, 47
  updating, 116
Norton AntiVirus Clinic, 113–119
Norton Backup, 120–147
  configuring, 9, 122–124
  installing, 6
  macros in, 145–147
  Restore window, 140–144
  running at shutdown, 45
  setup files for, 131–133
Norton Cache, 188–193
  configuring, 188–191
  installing, 7
  as startup program, 8, 47

uninstalling, 193
using, 192–193
Norton Commander Mail, importing from, 96
Norton Commander mode,
  210–212
Norton Configuration Pro-
  gram, installing, 7
Norton Desktop for DOS
  configuration, 18–47
  installing, 2–9
  memory for, 9–15
  starting Norton Menu from,
  102–103
  as startup program, 8, 47
Norton Desktop for Windows,
  and SmartCan, 194–195
Norton Disk Doctor, 147–152
  installing, 7
  running at shutdown, 45
  and Scheduler disabled, 154
  as startup program, 8, 46
  undoing changes, 151
Norton Mail, 91–102
  configuring, 92
  installing, 6
  receiving mail with, 99–100
  and Scheduler disabled, 154
  sending mail with, 101–102
Norton Menu, 102–111
Norton Unformat, 90. *See also*
  UnFormat
notes, attaching to calendar
  date, 85
.NPS file name extension, 31

O

Open (File menu), 56, 68, 103
Open Drive Window (Window
  menu), 75

Open Window (Window
  menu), 54
opening drive windows, 75
optimization of disks
  method, 157–158
  scheduling, 8
optimizing cache buffers, 191
Options menu
  Create Batch, 64
  Global, 117
  Match Upper/Lowercase, 61
  Page Width, 59–60
  Preferences, 103–104
  Search Sets, 63
orientation, for printer, 32
Out Folder, 92
output destination (Printer options), 31
overwriting files
  during restore, 144
  prompt before, 127
  prompt before backup, 130–
  131
  prompt during restore, 142

P

page size, 31
paged memory, 11
panes
  configuring, 78
  in drive window, 76
paper mail address type, 97–98
partition table
  repairing, 114
  restoring, 186
Partition Tables screen, 166
partition tests, skipping, 148
Password (Configure menu),
  26–27
passwords, 26–27

for backups, 126
for compressed files, 53
for MCI Mail account, 94
for menu items, 110–111
for Norton AntiVirus option,
  119
for Norton Menu, 102, 104,
  107
removing for menu, 111
for running batch files, 109
for screen saver, 41–42
in shutdown routine, 44
Paste (Edit menu), 58
pasting text, 58
PATH statement, adding ND
  directory to, 9
paths, for compressed files, 20
pause
  in batch-file execution, 65,
  202–203
  in macros, 146
  for program menu items, 108
PCX files, for Screen Saver, 42
Performance Index screen, 167
phone number, for MCI
  Telephone, 93
pipe character (|), 61–62
popup alert, for virus detection, 118
portrait orientation, 32
ports
  for Desktop Link, 21
  for modem, 93
Preconfigure options (Install
  program), 7–9
Preferences (Configure menu),
  27–30, 43, 210
preset program level
  for backup, 126
  for Compare window, 138

in Norton Backup, macros in, 145–146
for restoring backups, 141–142
Print (File menu), 58
Print Setup (File menu), 58
PRINTCHAR command (Batch Enhancer), 204
printers
  configuring, 30–32
  setup for Norton Mail, 96
printing
  catalogs, 140, 143
  files, 58, 68–69
  information screen, 165
  system summary report, 164–165
program level, for backup, 125–131
Program level dialog box (Norton Backup), 121
programs
  adding to menus, 106–108
  associating file name extensions with, 50–52
  changes in, 116
  delayed scheduled execution, 153
  in file pane, 78
  scheduling, 152
  searching text in, 61
  updates and inoculation data, 117
prompts
  for arguments, 108
  audible for backup, 129
  in batch files, 200–201
  before overwriting diskettes, 127
  before overwriting files during restore, 142

properties, of files, 69–70
Properties (File menu), 52, 69
proprietary diskette format, for backup, 127
Prune & Graft (Disk menu), 70
pruning directories, 70
pull-down menus
  adding custom items to, 36
  adding menu item to, 35
  adding to menu bar, 33–35
  configuring, 32–37
  editing or deleting items from, 36–37

Q

Quarterdeck Expanded Memory Manager386 (QEMM386), 12
Quattro Pro spreadsheet files
  extensions for, 51
  in file pane, 79
question mark (?) wildcard character, 61–62
Quick Format, 88–89

R

RAM drive, 14–15
Read-After-Write, for Speed Disk, 159
Read-ahead buffer, 190–191
README.TXT, 7
read-only files, 52
  backups and, 135
REBOOT command (Batch Enhancer), 204
rebooting computer, after defragmentation, 163
receiving mail, with Norton Mail, 99–100

Recover command (DOS), 184–185

reformatting disks, without data destruction, 186

reformatting text, 59–60

reinoculating files, 115

Rename (File menu), 71, 170

renaming, printer configuration file, 32

Replace (Search menu), 59

reply, to network message, 112

Reply (Mail menu), 100

reports
  on backup, 126–127, 130
  on compare operation, 139
  on file fragmentation, 161
  from Norton Cache, 193
  from Norton Disk Doctor, 149
  printing system summary, 164–165
  on restoring backups, 142
  on viruses, 118

rescue disk
  creating, 9, 183
  restoring, 185–186

Restore window, 140–144
  catalogs for, 143

root directory, saving, 187

ROWCOL command (Batch Enhancer), 205

.RPT file name extension, 127, 130

Run (File menu), 66

S

SA (Screen Attributes) command, 205–206

Safe format, 88, 188
  installing, 7

Save (File menu), 57

Save As (File menu), 57

Save System Files screen, 3

saving
  configuration, 43
  disk information, 187
  files, 57
  menus, 34–35
  Speed Disk configuration, 157

Scan menu
  Directory, 114
  Drive, 113
  File, 114

Scheduler, 100, 152–154
  adding event to, 153
  for automatic backups, 145
  removing events from, 154

Scheduler/Screen Saver
  installing, 6
  as startup program, 8, 47

screen
  batch command to clear, 202
  configuring, 37–40
  writing character to, 204

Screen Saver (Configure menu), 41

Screen Saver/Sleeper, configuring, 41–43

Search menu
  Continue Search, 170–171
  Find, 59
  For Data Types, 171
  For Lost Names, 172
  For Text, 171
  Go To, 73
  Replace, 59
  Set Search Range, 173

search sets, 63–64

searches
  for clusters in erased files, 175
  for deleted data fragments, 171

for files in erased directories, 172

for text on erased disk, 171–172

for text in files, 61

for text in viewer, 74

Select (File menu), 72

Select All (Edit menu), 58

Select Directory Order dialog box, 159

Select Group (File menu), 174

selecting files
for backup, 133–134
for compare, 139–140
in drive windows, 71–72

Send/Receive (Mail menu), 100, 102

sending mail, with Norton Mail, 101–102

sensitivity, of mouse, 24–25

serial cables, 86

Serve Remote Link (Disk menu), 86

server, 86

.SET file name extension, 133

Set Search Range (Search menu), 173

setup, for Norton Mail, 92–93

setup files, for backup, 131–133, 145

Setup menu
Import, 96
MCI Accounts, 94
Printer, for Norton Mail, 96

setup string, for modem, 94

shadows for windows, 28, 207

shell, installing Norton Menu as, 102

Shift key, status of, 206

SHIFTSTATE command (Batch Enhancer), 206

shortcut keys, assigning to menus, 34, 35

shrinking files, for compression, 20

shutdown options (Preferences), 28

shutdown routine, configuring, 43–45

SmartCan, 193–196
configuring for startup, 8, 47
installing, 7
purging files manually, 195–196
turning on and off, 196

Software Interrupts screen, 166

Sort By (View menu), 80

sort order
in file pane, 80
for files, 160, 163–164

sorting, file list, 172–173

sound, from modem, 93

Special Selections dialog box, for backup, 135

speed
of computer, 188
for Desktop Link, 22
of Norton Backup, 124

Speed Disk, 155–164
installing, 7
optimization method, 157–158
options, 158–159
running at shutdown, 45
and Scheduler disabled, 154
unmovable files in, 160–161

Speed Search, 159, 161, 169

Speed Search Box, in drive window, 76–77

Speed Search Preview, 28

spreadsheet data
search erased disk for, 171
searching text in, 61

STACKER drive, Norton Anti-Virus and, 120
starting Norton Menu
  from command line, 103
  from Norton Desktop, 102–103
startup
  automatic for Norton Desktop, 8
  configuring, 45–47
  configuring Image for, 8
  configuring Norton Disk Doctor for, 8
  configuring SmartCan for, 8
  for screen saver/sleeper, 41
Startup Programs (Configure menu), 45, 192
static file list, viewing, 162
statistics, in backup report, 130
status bar, in drive window, 76
storage method, for file compression, 20
style options (Preferences), 28
subdirectories
  creating, 67
  deleting, 55–56
  drag & drop and, 28
  renaming, 71
  scanning for viruses, 114
submenus, 106
  adding, 108
SuperFind window, 60–65
surface tests, 147, 149, 150
  skipping, 148
swap files, RAM drive for, 14
Symantec BBS, virus definition files from, 115
SYS command (DOS), 91, 184

system diskettes, formatting, 12
system files, 52
  backups and, 135
  in file pane, 79
System Information, 164–168
  installing, 7
system summary report, printing, 164–165
System Summary screen, 166

T

tagging files, for unerasure, 173
tape drives
  appending backup data to, 128
  configuring for Norton Backup, 123
  for Norton Backup, 120, 121
  testing, 122
telecommunications programs, disabling screen saver during, 42
Telex address type, 98
terminate-and-stay-resident programs. *See* memory-resident programs
tests
  by Norton Backup, 120, 121, 123–124
  skipping in Norton Disk Doctor, 148
text
  color of, 205
  deleting, 59
  reformatting, 59–60
  searching file for, 61
text attributes, for custom messages, 148

time
  for compressed file, 20
  displaying for file creation, 79
  sorting files by, 163
timeouts, network, 26
titles of menus, changing, 103
tools, installing, 6–7
Tools menu
  Calculator, 84
  Calendar, 85
  Edit, 103
  Menu, 102
  Network Message, 111
  Norton AntiVirus, 113
  Norton Backup, 120–122
  Norton Disk Doctor, 147
  Scheduler, 100, 152
  Speed Disk, 155
  Uninoculate, 117
Tree pane
  in Select Backup Files win-
    dow, 133
  Speed Search box for, 77
Tree Pane (View menu), 70, 72,
  78
TRIGGER command (Batch En-
  hancer), 206
TSR Programs screen, 167
TSRs. *See* memory-resident
  programs
.TXT file name extension, 171

U

unattended backup, 126
unattended compare, 138
unattended restore, 142
uncompressing files, 54
undeleting addresses, 99

UnErase, 168–179
  automatic, 174–177
  installing, 7
  and Scheduler disabled, 154
  SmartCan and, 193
  tagging files for, 173
  tagging group of files for, 174
unerased files
  new location for, 177
  new name for, 176–177
UnFormat, 90, 196–197
  installing, 7
  and Scheduler disabled, 154
uninstalling, Norton Cache, 193
unknown viruses
  detecting, 118
  inoculation against, 116–117
unmovable files
  list of, 162
  in Speed Disk, 160–161
Unselect Group (File menu),
  177
untagging files, 177–178
unused space, clearing by
  Speed Disk, 159
updating, Norton AntiVirus,
  116
upper memory area, 10–11

V

verifying
  backup data, 126
  restore data, 142
Video and Mouse Configuration dialog box, 121
Video/Mouse (Configure
  menu), 24, 37–40
Video Summary screen, 166

View (File menu), 74

View All Directories (File menu), 170

View Current Directory (File menu), 170

View menu
  DOS Background, 40, 66
  File Details, 79
  Filter, 78–79
  Refresh, 77
  Sort By, 80
  Tree Pane, 70, 72
  Viewer ➤ Go To, 73

View pane, configuring, 78

Viewers
  installing, 6
  search for text in, 74

viewing
  compressed file contents, 54
  data as ASCII characters, 176
  data as hex characters, 176
  disk information, 162
  file contents from file lists, 178
  file information, 178
  files, 72–75
  graphic files, 74–75
  information screen, 166–167
  map legend, 162
  MCI Mail accounts, 95–96
  scheduled events list, 152
  static file list, 162

Virus Definition Update Disk Service, 116

virus definitions, updating, 115–116

virus intercept, 8

viruses
  inoculation against unknown, 116–117
  protection against, 112

scanning for at startup, 8

W

Wait… message, 30

Walk Map (Information menu), 162–163

WEEKDAY command (Batch Enhancer), 206–207

wildcard characters, 61–62

WINDOW command (Batch Enhancer), 207

Window menu
  Compare Windows, 81
  Open Drive Window, 75
  Open Window, 54

windows. *See also* drive windows
  shadows on, 28, 207

Windows (Microsoft)
  creating group for Desktop, 9
  Norton Cache and, 191

.WK1 file name extension, 171

word wrap, 31

WordStar data format, 31

workstations, names, 26

Write-back buffer, 191

write requests, background processing of, 190

writing messages, for MCI Mail, 101–102

X

XT computers, memory on, 11

Z

.ZIP file name extension, 53

zooming boxes, 38

Selections from The SYBEX Library

UTILITIES

The Computer Virus Protection Handbook
Colin Haynes
192pp. Ref. 696-0
This book is the equivalent of an intensive emergency preparedness seminar on computer viruses. Readers learn what viruses are, how they are created, and how they infect systems. Step-by-step procedures help computer users to identify vulnerabilities, and to assess the consequences of a virus infection. Strategies on coping with viruses, as well as methods of data recovery, make this book well worth the investment.

Mastering the Norton Utilities 5
Peter Dyson
400pp, Ref. 725-8
This complete guide to installing and using the Norton Utilities 5 is a must for beginning and experienced users alike. It offers a clear, detailed description of each utility, with options, uses and examples— so users can quickly identify the programs they need and put Norton right to work. Includes valuable coverage of the newest Norton enhancements.

Mastering PC Tools Deluxe 6
For Versions 5.5 and 6.0
425pp, Ref. 700-2
An up-to-date guide to the lifesaving utilities in PC Tools Deluxe version 6.0 from installation, to high-speed back-ups, data recovery, file encryption, desktop applications, and more. Includes detailed background on DOS and hardware such as floppies, hard disks, modems and fax cards.

Norton Desktop for Windows Instant Reference
Sharon Crawford
Charlie Russell
200pp; Ref. 894-7
For anyone using Norton's version of the Windows desktop, here's a compact, fast-access guide to every feature of the package—from file management functions, to disaster prevention tools, configuration commands, batch language extensions, and more. Concise, quick-reference entries are alphabetized by topic, and include practical tips and examples.

Norton Utilities 5 Instant Reference
Michael Gross
162pp. Ref. 737-1
Organized alphabetically by program name, this pocket-sized reference offers complete information on each utility in the Norton 5 package—including a descriptive summary, exact syntax, command line options, brief explanation, and examples. Gives proficient users a quick reminder, and helps with unfamiliar options.

Norton Utilities 6 Instant Reference
Michael Gross
175pp; Ref. 865-3
This pocket-size guide to Norton Utilities 6 provides fast answers when and where they're needed. Reference entries are organized alphabetically by program name, and provide a descriptive summary, exact syntax, command line options, brief explanations, and examples. For a quick reminder, or help with unfamiliar options.

PC Tools Deluxe 6 Instant Reference
Gordon McComb
194pp. Ref. 728-2

Keep this one handy for fast access to quick reminders and essential information on the latest PC Tools Utilities. Alphabetical entries cover all the Tools of Version 6—from data recovery to desktop applications—with concise summaries, syntax, options, brief explanations, and examples.

Understanding Norton Desktop for Windows
Peter Dyson
500pp; Ref. 888-2

This detailed, hands-on guide shows how to make the most of Norton's powerful Windows Desktop—to make Windows easier to use, customize and optimize the environment, take advantage of shortcuts, improve disk management, simplify disaster recovery, and more. Each program in the Norton Desktop gets thorough treatment, with plenty of practical examples.

Understanding the Norton Utilities 6 (Second Edition)
Peter Dyson
500pp; Ref. 855-6

Here is a detailed, practical sourcebook for PC users seeking to streamline their computing and extend the power of DOS with Norton 6. Features hands-on examples and up-to-date coverage of such topics as file management and security, hard disk maintenance, disaster recovery, and batch programming. Includes a complete command guide.

Understanding PC Tools 7
Peter Dyson
500pp; Ref. 850-5

Turn here for a complete guide to taking advantage of the new version of PC Tools for DOS 5 and Windows—with hands-on coverage of everything from installation to telecommunications. Special topics include networking; data security and encryption; virus detection; remote computing; and many new options for disk maintenance, disaster prevention, and data recovery.

Up & Running with Carbon Copy Plus
Marvin Bryan
124pp. Ref. 709-6

A speedy, thorough introduction to Carbon Copy Plus, for controlling remote computers from a PC. Coverage is in twenty time-coded "steps"—lessons that take 15 minutes to an hour to complete. Topics include program set-up, making and receiving calls, file transfer, security, terminal emulation, and using Scripts.

Up & Running with Norton Desktop for Windows
Michael Gross
David Clark
140pp; Ref. 885-8

Norton's new desktop utility package lets you customize Windows to your heart's content. Don't miss out! Learn to use this versatile program in just 20 basic lessons. Each lesson takes less than an hour to complete, and wastes no time on unnecessary detail.

Up & Running with Norton Utilities 5
Michael Gross
154pp. Ref. 819-0

Get a fast jump on Norton Utilties 5. In just 20 lessons, you can learn to retrieve erased files, password protect and encrypt your data, make your system work faster, unformat accidentally formatted disks, find "lost" files on your hard disk, and reconstruct damaged files.

Up & Running with Norton Utilities 6
Michael Gross
140pp; Ref. 874-2

Come up to speed with Norton Utilities 6 in just 20 steps. This slim volume covers all of Norton's constituent programs (for both versions 5 and 6), provides command line syntax and options, and spells out the differences between versions 5 and 6 with special upgrade notes.

Up & Running with PC Tools Deluxe 6
Thomas Holste
180pp. Ref.678-2
Learn to use this software program in just 20 basic steps. Readers get a quick, inexpensive introduction to using the Tools for disaster recovery, disk and file management, and more.

Up & Running with XTreeGold 2
Robin Merrin
136pp. Ref. 820-3
Covers both XTreeGold 2 and XTreePro-Gold 1. In just 20 steps, each taking no more than 15 minutes to an hour, you can learn to customize your display, archive files, navigate the user interface, copy and back up your files, undelete accidentally erased files, and more.

WORD PROCESSING

The ABC's of Microsoft Word (Third Edition)
Alan R. Neibauer
461pp. Ref. 604-9
This is for the novice WORD user who wants to begin producing documents in the shortest time possible. Each chapter has short, easy-to-follow lessons for both keyboard and mouse, including all the basic editing, formatting and printing functions. Version 5.0.

The ABC's of Microsoft Word for Windows
Alan R. Neibauer
334pp. Ref. 784-6
Designed for beginning Word for Windows users, as well as for experienced Word users who are changing from DOS to the Windows version. Covers everything from typing, saving, and printing your first document, to creating tables, equations, and graphics.

The ABC's of WordPerfect 5
Alan R. Neibauer
283pp. Ref. 504-2
This introduction explains the basics of desktop publishing with WordPerfect 5: editing, layout, formatting, printing, sorting, merging, and more. Readers are shown how to use WordPerfect 5's new features to produce great-looking reports.

The ABC's of WordPerfect 5.1 for Windows
Alan R. Neibauer
350pp; Ref. 803-3
This highly praised beginner's tutorial is now in a special new edition for Word-Perfect 5.1 for Windows—featuring WYSI-WYG graphics, font preview, the button bar, and more. It covers all the essentials of word processing, from basic editing to simple desktop publishing, in short, easy-to-follow lessons. Suitable for first-time computer users.

The ABC's of WordPerfect 5.1
Alan R. Neibauer
352pp. Ref. 672-3
Neibauer's delightful writing style makes this clear tutorial an especially effective learning tool. Learn all about 5.1's new drop-down menus and mouse capabilities that reduce the tedious memorization of function keys.

The Complete Guide to MultiMate
Carol Holcomb Dreger
208pp. Ref. 229-9
This step-by-step tutorial is also an excellent reference guide to MultiMate features and uses. Topics include search/replace, library and merge functions, repagination, document defaults and more.